HELP
OTHE
━━━━━━━━━━━━━━ • CRISIS •
SUBSTANCE ABUSE

WILLIAM DAVIS, PSY. D
PATRICIA MYERS, M.S.
MARION DUCKWORTH

David C. Cook Publishing Co.
Elgin, Illinois—Weston, Ontario

Author's note: This book does not constitute mental health treatment or legal counsel, and should not be considered a substitute for professional help. Neither the authors nor the publisher can be held liable for any act or failure to act upon the information contained herein.

The identities of people whose stories are contained in this book have been altered to protect their anonymity, except where their stories are a matter of public record and proceeding.

David C. Cook Publishing Co.
Elgin, Illinois—Weston, Ontario
Substance Abuse
© 1990 David C. Cook Publishing Co.

All rights reserved. Except for brief excerpts for review purposes, no part of this book may be reproduced or used in any form without written permission from the publisher.

Scripture quotations, unless otherwise noted, are from the *Holy Bible: New International Version.* © 1973, 1978, 1984 by the New York International Bible Society. Used by permission of Zondervan Bible Publishers.

The artwork on the cover of this book is for illustrative purposes only. It does not depict actual persons engaged in the situations described in this book, nor is it intended to do so.

Published by David C. Cook Publishing Co.
850 N. Grove Ave., Elgin, IL 60120
Cable Address: DCCOOK
Designed by Christopher Patchel
Photo by Tammie Edington
Illustrated by Stephen D. Smith
Printed in the United States of America
Library of Congress Catalog Card Number: 90-82863

ISBN: 1-55513-011-9

CONTENTS

INTRODUCTION

Some Thoughts by William Davis, Psy. D.

Few of the problems I've confronted in the lives of people during fourteen years as a professional counselor and twelve years as a teaching elder in my church have been more devastating than the trauma of addiction. During the years I was director of counseling for a drop-in crisis center for addicts, I confronted it head-on, day after day as we worked to get them off the street and into treatment and recovery.

As a result, I have become convinced that addiction imprisons the soul because it takes total control of the individual. The addict's whole life revolves around the drug. Relationships, jobs—everything is expendable. It keeps the person from growing mentally, emotionally, spiritually, and socially. It steals one's very identity. Furthermore, everyone close to the addict is marked with pain.

I haven't been able to walk away unaffected by the misery drug use has caused my clients. It has made me angry; it has caused me to grieve.

But knowing that there is a way out of the hell that addiction creates—and that Christians can play a key role— compels me to write this book.

My aim has been to provide you with tools to help you encourage sufferers to seek the path out of the entrapment they're in. It's my hope that, by using these tools, you'll be able to reduce the number of people affected by addiction in your congregation and in the community around you.

When someone seeks help because he or she is truly

exhausted by the pain and struggle, assure that person that help is available. When someone can't muster courage to go on, assure him or her that God is ready to provide strength.

Some Thoughts by Patricia Myers, M.S.

In my practice, I've counseled children of alcoholics, whole families, and addicted teenagers in a treatment center. Now I'm in private practice, and part of my work is to help clients who have addiction-related problems.

But the cases hardest to put out of my mind are those of kids—as young as three years old—who've been damaged due to parental drug and alcohol addiction. For some of them the damage will be permanent because they won't have the long-term treatment it takes to recover. They may even become addicts themselves as a result. It's these young, innocent victims that have motivated me to contribute to this book.

I've tried to emphasize that addiction and its effects is a complex subject and there are no easy answers. Too often I've heard remarks by Christians intimating that, "If you had more faith, God would take care of your problem," or "Just read your Bible more and pray more, and you'll be okay."

That's laying more guilt at the feet of those who are already struggling under the heavy load of addiction and its ripple effects. When we do that, we widen the schism they feel exists between themselves and God. Instead of widening the schism, let's help close it. What these individuals need to know is that God is approachable, that He does care, that He is willing to answer prayer—and that we are not going to walk away from them in the meantime.

Therefore, we, as loving brothers and sisters, need to educate ourselves so we can meet their needs. I pray that this book will be used to do that.

Some Thoughts by Marion Duckworth

As an author, speaker, and lay counselor, I'm one of the

people who has badly needed a book like this. Two incidents are most vivid in my mind.

The first took place several years ago when a woman came to me because she had serious personal problems. Books I'd written led her to believe I'd understand.

She and I met weekly for months, and she talked about how hard it was for her to cope and what the reasons were. I tried to help her. But the snow melted and the crocuses appeared before she finally admitted that she'd been addicted to barbiturates for a considerable length of time.

The second incident took place years before that when, with my husband, I was a stateside missionary. In one small town where we ministered, it was no secret that the husband and father of a certain family was an alcoholic. I visited his wife and brought clothing and food and whatever comfort I could. But I knew it wasn't nearly enough. Here was a family to whom the poverty level would have seemed like awesome wealth. Here were children who wore a pinched, pale look, like young plants that had been deprived of light and sun.

One night, too drunk to drive, the alcoholic father put his oldest child behind the wheel to take the two of them home. Inexperienced, the youth lost control, and the car crashed. The child was killed. His father survived. Some time after we moved away, we heard that the experience had straightened the father out.

Could I have helped the people involved in these two incidents sooner, been more effective, spared them some misery if I'd known more? I honestly believe I could have.

That's why it's been important for me to work on this book —so we in the church will have that information. The guidelines that Bill Davis and Pat Myers have provided are exactly what I need. It could be that they're exactly what you need, too.

CHAPTER ONE

THE PROBLEM OF
SUBSTANCE ABUSE

IT'S NOT AN OVERSTATEMENT TO SAY THAT WE'RE A DRUG-dependent society. Consider the average home: first thing in the morning, the bleary-eyed residents stumble into the kitchen and grope for a cup of coffee. It's probably only the first of several doses of caffeine—a stimulant drug —in the form of more coffee or tea or soft drinks that day when the spirit is willing but the body is definitely weak.

As tensions mount, the same individuals pop aspirin or other headache remedies when exercise or a more realistic schedule might have provided relief the healthy way. Simultaneously, they may also be puffing on another drug of choice—nicotine, in the form of tobacco. At bedtime, they may reach for an over-the-counter preparation to help them sleep.

Depending on drugs has become a way of life that's hyped by the media. Viewers are entertained by sitcoms and films and stand-up comics that depict the careless use of chemicals. Commercials between programs further entice people to use alcohol to have more fun. In spite of recent anti-drug campaigns featuring celebrities, the media milieu still provides broad support for the abuse of substances that wreak havoc in the lives of millions of people.

Present but Invisible Sufferers

Those affected aren't only street people who wear thrift shop clothing and drink cheap wine in alleys, or party-types who snort cocaine with friends and boast that they divorced themselves from organized religion long ago. Dressed in

9

designer jeans or business suits and fine dresses, substance abusers sit in our church pews and Sunday school chairs—silent sufferers who desperately need our help.

But because they're silent and successful at hiding their secret, they blend in with the other smiling, polished worshipers. So a church leader or member may conclude that, except for rare cases, individuals who abuse chemicals exist "out there"—outside church doors and not "in here."

The facts prove otherwise. Substance abusers populate our churches in surprising numbers; their problems are just invisible to most of us. Consider the following examples.

LuAnn: Turned on in Youth Group

LuAnn was in church regularly. She made the effort even though no one else in her family attended.

As a teenager, she'd been a leader in her youth group for a couple of years when a guy caught her eye. He was also a member of the youth group, but he used alcohol. "To be his girlfriend," LuAnn recalls, "I did what he and his crowd did. That meant getting drunk every weekend and sometimes more often. I had low self-esteem and thought I was homely, and here was this male attention with tenderness and touching—things that were foreign to me. That pretty much took my focus off the Lord."

By the time LuAnn was sixteen she and her boyfriend broke up. Later she met and married a rock musician. In addition to alcohol, she began smoking pot and using hallucinogens like LSD and mescaline. The next few years were a roller coaster of addictive behavior.

A crisis would shake her so badly that she'd try to stay clean and sober. During those periods, she'd turn to God and resume church attendance. But no one in the churches LuAnn attended knew about her problem any more than they had when she was a teenager; like most addicts, she was secretive about it. As a result, she drifted in and out of church. Something would trigger the use of drugs and alcohol again; she'd fall away from the Lord.

It happened, for example, after she moved to another city. Everything seemed strange—even the new church she began attending. First she reverted to her old habit of smoking cigarettes as a way to deal with the stress. Soon, she brought some beer home and it didn't take long for her to start smoking marijuana. She stopped going to church and lived to get high. "It became a predictable pattern," she says.

Gordon: Well-Grounded in the Church

Gordon's addiction began in high school, too. Raised in a stable Christian home, he attended church regularly and acquired a lapel full of perfect attendance pins. But unlike his siblings, Gordon was a rebel: "As a teenager, I got drunk a couple of weekends a month and drank even more when I got out of high school."

When he returned from serving in Vietnam—where he had started using drugs—he was even more rebellious. "I didn't recover for a long time. Drinking and using created chaos in my life, and the more it created, the more I consumed as an escape."

He says now that he came to know Jesus Christ as a teenager but dropped out of church during those years. He sometimes attended other churches as an adult when he was trying to remain clean and sober, but that never lasted long. Like LuAnn, he was secretive about his addiction, and no one in pew or pulpit knew. So when he succumbed to the temptation to drink and use drugs again, others in the church were completely unaware.

Sandi: Abused by a Drinking Father

Sandi, an attractive woman in her thirties, attended church regularly with her whole family from the time she was small. When her dad started drinking and dropped out of church, she and the others in her family kept attending.

"No one in our church knew what was going on," she recalls. But the misery she suffered silently was enormous. Before her dad began drinking, for example, "we would have stimulating conversation at the dinner table. But suddenly everything changed. He was argumentative—especially with me. No matter what I said, he put me down.

"There was a look in his eyes that said, 'You are dirt.' I'd go to my room and cry and cry." She suffered through those years alone, and it wasn't until she was in her late twenties that she realized it was alcohol that caused her pain.

Evidence in Our Churches

These stories and the others in this book are only examples of a much larger problem in our churches. How do we know? For one thing, consider the fact that social drinking is more acceptable in many Christian circles today than it has been. So it follows that more in all age groups will fall into alcoholism. Just being Christians doesn't make us invulnerable to addiction.

Another evidence is the growing number of support groups churches are sponsoring for alcoholics, drug addicts, spouses of addicts, and their families. That's because the need among Christians is great and church staff members realize they must do something about it.

The First Evangelical Free Church of Fullerton, California, where Charles Swindoll is senior pastor, has groups to minister to cocaine users, adolescent substance abusers, alcohol abusers, female alcohol abusers, codependents (people who organize their lives, beliefs, actions, values, and decisions around other people's addictions), and adult children of alcoholics. The church has a list of over four hundred Christian support groups in the United States alone for adult children of dysfunctional families (families where healthy relationships and patterns have been destroyed by addictions or other negative behavior). The California-based Overcomer's Outreach now numbers six hundred support groups that serve drug and alcohol abusers. (Those with other kinds of addictions like gambling or sex are welcome to attend, too.)

Overcomers Outreach was founded in 1985 by former addict Bob Bartosch and his wife Pauline. The organization describes itself in its booklet, *Freed*, as "a bridge between Twelve Step groups and the church . . . a ministry that provides Christian resources, education through workshops and written materials, and tools to initiate and maintain Twelve Step support groups."

Keep in mind that every family member is scarred by the presence of an addict and that addiction can affect generations. Suppose Keith is an addict. He doesn't attend your church, but his children do. Because of his influence, they are in danger of becoming addicts themselves. Even if they don't, they will face other problems in developing healthy personalities. And *they* sit in your pews.

If the second generation remains untreated, the third generation—their children who, let us say, also attend church —are also more likely to abuse substances or have family problems because they haven't learned how to relate to other people in healthy ways.

We also know that this problem is common behind our stained glass walls because Christian counselors work with a significant number of substance abusers who are part of the church. Clients often include youth who smoke pot and drink beer, and adults—particularly women—who are addicted to some tranquilizing agent. But those who seek help are undoubtedly only the tip of the iceberg.

Alcohol is the most abused drug in society today, according to a Louis Harris poll. In the United States alone there are approximately ten million alcoholics. Two-thirds of all adults know someone who is a problem drinker.

Statistics for the number of drug abusers are harder to come by, but it's estimated that there are as many as 6.5 million addicts who need drug rehabilitation. In 1987, 937,000 drug abuse violations were reported by law enforcement agencies to the FBI. According to one survey, one in four drivers killed in auto accidents was found to have used cocaine in the preceding twenty-four hours.

No one is counting the number of people who are smoking marijuana, shooting heroin, and swallowing amphetamines and tranquilizers with the shades drawn. One recent survey did report that one in eighteen high school seniors has tried crack and the number has risen dramatically since then. In 1989, the National Institute on Drug Abuse estimated that 862,000 Americans used cocaine frequently, mainly in the form of crack, but a more recent study found that at least 1.3 million additional Americans now may be current users of the drug.[1]

The national drug abuse problem has been called an epidemic, a plague, and a scourge by political candidates who know they must make the drug war a priority in their campaigns. On nearly any day in any major newspaper, one can find at least one article on the subject. And it's an unusual news day when the TV networks don't include it in their half-hour evening broadcasts.

The Cost in Human Misery

When we consider the pain and suffering drug and alcohol addiction is causing, we realize how imperative it is to help those in our churches. Consider the following:

• *The effect on the abuser.* If the individual keeps using his or her substance of choice, physical, mental, emotional, and spiritual deterioration will ensue. Eventually, the habit can kill the abuser.

• *The effect on the family.* Parents who have grappled with the addiction of a son or daughter call it the worst

14

experience of their lives. So have grown children who have watched helplessly while parents destroy themselves. *Newsweek* states that more than 28 million in the U. S. have had an alcoholic parent.

• *Babies may be the most innocent victims of all.* Between 4,000 and 8,000 babies are born each year with Fetal Alcohol Syndrome because the mother has consumed beverage alcohol during pregnancy. Fetal Alcohol Syndrome can damage the baby's central nervous system, causing deficiencies in growth, mental retardation, facial abnormalities, and other birth defects. An additional 11,000 to 19,000 babies are born each year with at least some damage from prenatal alcohol consumption.

The number of babies born to drug-addicted mothers has increased three to four times in recent years. Typically, these infants cry, scream inconsolably, and scratch their faces as helpers rock, croon, feed, and walk them during their first four to six weeks of misery. These babies exist wherever there are pregnant addicts who haven't curbed their habit.

• *Children of addicted parents.* Sons of alcoholic fathers have a four-times greater risk of becoming alcoholic than those not raised by one. Daughters whose mothers are alcoholic stand a three-times greater risk of alcoholism.

In addition, these children are often emotionally and/or physically abused. They have a three-times greater risk of dropping out of school or being expelled. A large number will seek psychological treatment for depression and anxiety.

• *Strangers also suffer.* Drunk and drug-intoxicated drivers maim, paralyze, and kill strangers as well as acquaintances. Citizens lose valuable property through robberies and burglaries because addicts need money to buy drugs. Innocent victims are caught in drug-war crossfire, like the eight-year-old child from Philadelphia who will spend his life in a wheelchair because he was hit by a stray bullet. A significant number of people lose their lives due to drug- and alcohol-related homicides—and these are on the increase.

• *The cost in dollars and cents is staggering.* Nine hundred million dollars was approved by Congress in 1989 for treatment programs alone—and that's in addition to state and local spending. Companies lose about $33 billion a year from lowered output, on-the-job accidents, theft, and security breeches—all traceable to substance abuse.

Alcohol and Its Effects

Because the manufacture, sale, and consumption of beverage alcohol is legal and socially acceptable, it is not always thought of as a drug. But that's exactly what it is, because it contains ethyl alcohol or ethanol, a mood-altering substance.

Beer and wine are no less harmful than whiskey. A 4.5 percent, sixteen-ounce glass of beer, a five-ounce glass of wine, and a one-and-a-half-ounce shot glass of hundred-proof whiskey each contain about three-fourths ounce of alcohol. So individuals who say, "I can't be (or become) addicted because I only drink beer (or wine)" are fooling themselves. (Specific figures depend on the alcohol content of each beverage.)

The first drink of alcohol acts as a stimulant, but when more is consumed, the alcohol depresses parts of the brain. As a result, the drinker may weave when he or she walks and slur his or her speech. Judgment and coordination are affected. As more is consumed, the individual may sleep, laugh or cry uncontrollably, or become antagonistic.

When the drinker's blood alcohol level rises even more, he or she falls into a stupor. If the level reaches .4 or .5 percent, the person lapses into a coma. Still higher levels can suppress breathing and heartbeat and cause death.

The more alcohol an individual uses over a period of time, the greater his or her tolerance to it will be and the more he or she will require to produce the same result. Vision, muscular control, memory loss and performance, liver damage, and other evidences of physical deterioration are only some of the long-term effects.

Drugs and Their Effects

What physical symptoms can a youth leader expect to see in a teen who is using marijuana? Or what signs might a pastor see in an adult who is using amphetamines?

The following list describes the effects of the most often abused drugs. Variables, such as the amount consumed and how many kinds are used, are determining factors.

Marijuana: drowsiness, excitement and hyperactivity, irritability and restlessness, anxiety, euphoria, depression, hallucinations, panic, talkativeness, laughter, impairment of coordination, inflamed eyes, increased appetite, distortion of space or time.

Heroin: drowsiness, anxiety, euphoria, slurred speech, impaired coordination, depressed reflexes, constricted pupils, loss of appetite.

Cocaine and crack: excitability and hyperactivity, irritability and restlessness, anxiety, euphoria, hallucinations, talkativeness, tremor, hyperactive reflexes, dilated pupils, loss of appetite, insomnia.

Amphetamines or uppers: excitability and hyperactivity, irritability and restlessness, anxiety and euphoria, hallucinations, panic, talkativeness, tremor, dizziness, hyperactive reflexes, increased sweating, dilated pupils, unusually bright or shiny eyes, loss of appetite, and insomnia.

Methamphetamines, speed, or crank: same as amphetamines except for insomnia.

Inhalants (airplane glue): Poor motor coordination, impaired vision, impaired memory and thinking, violence.

Inhalants (amyl and butyl nitrites): slowed thought and headaches.

Barbiturates: drowsiness, irritability and restlessness, belligerence, euphoria, depression, irrational behavior, confusion, slurred speech, laughter, staggering, impairment of coordination, depressed reflexes, constricted pupils.

Lysergic acid diethylamide (LSD): excitation and hyperactivity, anxiety, euphoria, depression, hallucination, panic, irrational behavior, rambling speech, tremor, increased sweating, dilated pupils, distortion of space or time.

MDA, MDMA, ecstasy: excitation and hyperactivity, irritability and restlessness, euphoria, hallucinations, talkativeness, tremor, hyperactive reflexes, constricted pupils.

Phencyclidine (PCP): drowsiness, anxiety, panic, confusion, laughter, dizziness, impairment of coordination.

Ice (a smokable form of speed): lack of sleep and appetite and a feeling of increased energy. Increased use causes lethargy, weight loss, increased agitation, and ultimately paranoia and hallucinations.[2]

Answer Their SOS

In the past, church leaders were likely to get involved in an alcohol-related family problem only when the situation became acute. If a husband became violent, the police might be called, and the terrified wife may have contacted her pastor for help.

Clearly, we cannot wait to help until that kind of crisis occurs.

• First, we must devote ourselves to prevention. That means giving youth and adults the facts before they become hooked. It also means putting into action programs to grow addiction-free families. To help you do that, we have provided guidelines in Chapter 6.

• Second, helpers need to intervene in the lives of substance abusers and their loved ones. A youth leader could confront a teenager regarding the teen's use of pot, for instance, and show the young person and the family where to go for help. A pastor may confront an adult who gets drunk on periodic business trips and work with him or her to achieve sobriety. Counseling outlines in Chapters 3—5 will help you do that.

• Third, churches must seize ways to support addicts and their families as they recover. Chapter 6 will suggest ways to do that.

This three-pronged approach, soundly rooted in the love and truth of God, is one important way that we can present every person mature in Christ.

CHAPTER TWO

CASE STUDIES

T HESE CASE STUDIES ARE EXAMPLES OF THE KINDS OF SITU-
ations you may encounter. Each abuser and his or
her family is unique, of course. But there are common
denominators that can provide insights into the addicts and
families that you will meet. To gain the maximum benefit
from these case studies, ask yourself the following questions.

• What prompted the person to use drugs or alcohol?

• How did the person's habit cause him or her to deteriorate?

• In what ways did the addict's behavior affect family
members? How did each respond?

• How did family members help or hinder the addict?

• What was the crisis that caused the troubled individuals
to get or accept help?

• Who intervened and how?

• How did Christians help or hinder?

• What kind of treatment was effective?

The following accounts are true. Dan, Rosa, Mary, and
Ruth have related their painful experiences honestly—
telling it all—so you can get inside their skin. It's their
prayer that, as a result of hearing their stories, you'll be able
to help others.

An Addict in the Parsonage

The first time Dan got drunk, he was at home in the
parsonage basement. Thirteen years old and the son of a
minister, he and his stepbrother found some lemon extract
and had a contest to see who could drink the most at one

time. They finished off the seemingly-innocent little bottle, which was ninety-six percent alcohol.

Getting drunk seemed like a positive experience at the time, recalls Dan. It desensitized him to the confusion tearing at him over the death of his mother the year before, and it dulled his anger at his father's subsequent remarriage.

"Through high school, I drank whatever I could get." But Dan's double life—one as the obedient preacher's kid who was a youth group faithful and the other as the mainstay in the party crowd that drank to get intoxicated—had a high price. By the time he was sixteen, Dan required treatment for ulcers that had developed partly from worrying that his drinking would be found out. He also suffered frequent headaches.

As PKs (preacher's kids), he and his siblings were expected to maintain a strict standard. "We didn't get credit when we did things right, and we were told when we did things wrong. I heard constantly from my stepmother that what I did reflected on my father."

During high school, Dan started using all kinds of drugs. By the time he was a senior, he was experimenting with heroin and now considers himself addicted to drugs during those years.

When his father confronted him with information that Dan had used MDA (a drug known as "ecstasy" since it's been synthesized), he told his dad it was the first time he'd used any drugs and that he didn't even get high. "He accepted my story, but I felt tremendous guilt and sorrow for hurting him."

That night, Dan attempted suicide using MDA. "I almost died. The next morning, I barely made it upstairs (my stepbrother and I lived in a basement apartment of the parsonage). I was shaking too badly to hold a glass or shave. I had sores all over my mouth, had chewed my tongue all up, and had boils all over my chest.

"But I made it to family devotions, which we had precisely at seven every morning. My stepbrother shook his head in unbelief as my father read the Bible, because he knew I was barely able to function. But neither of my parents noticed."

After his high school graduation in 1971, Dan volunteered to go to Vietnam. He managed to stay clean all through basic and advanced training. But drugs were readily available, and he began using them again and was getting drunk, too.

Dan's world fell apart when he was transferred back to the States unexpectedly and found that his impending marriage was off. "I lost all respect for myself and didn't care. That's when I started using very heavily."

He knew if he continued, he'd kill himself. Now out of the Army and employed in one of a series of jobs, he heard about a Bible study held by a communal Christian household and attended it one night. "Their acceptance of me without judgment had a powerful effect. I'd had that kind of support from [fellow users] for years, but the more drug-affected we became, the more our relationships deteriorated.

"The next few months, I studied the Bible. When I decided that the promises were true, I made a commitment to Jesus Christ. Immediately, my physical craving for narcotics was gone. It was absolutely miraculous."

Dan called his parents to tell them the wonderful news, and, as a private ceremony he still recalls as deeply significant, he broke his favorite syringe.

Later Dan had a conversation with his dad about past addictive experiences. But his father was "heavily into denial, and I don't think he really believed what I said."

Dan had been delivered from drug addiction, but he reasoned that using alcohol was okay—that he could drink in moderation. What he'd done, however, was to transfer his dependency to that substance. "For the next nine years, it was a constant battle of not drinking, wishing I could drink, drinking and feeling guilty and out-of-control and preoccupied with the next time I could drink."

By 1984 Dan was married, the father of a son, a graduate from seminary, and serving as a youth pastor. He was even part of a team for drug and alcohol abuse intervention at the local high school. It was the training sessions for this team that forced him to confront his personal condition. "My denial was pretty well shattered. Admitting I had an alcohol problem was devastating." He became very depressed.

Dan's physician intervened in the situation together with Dan's wife, Chris, and other friends. Finally, Dan agreed to go to a treatment center. "It was one of the most painful experiences of my life but also one of the most important."

When Dan entered treatment, his dad finally believed his son was an addict. He told Dan, "I want to be there for you," but then he begged off attending a meeting at the treatment center the very next day because of "other things he had to do." The center was secular but several key personnel were Christians, so their approach was from a biblical perspective. After twenty-eight days, Dan was released and his church welcomed him back on staff and lovingly helped him through the transition period. He has since resigned that position and accepted one as associate pastor in another city where he recently celebrated four continuous years of sobriety.

The Child of an Alcoholic

Now in her mid-thirties, Rosa says her father's alcoholism was simply not talked about at home. "At first he'd only go on binges a couple of times a year—'when the crazies would come on,' as he put it.

"He heard voices, and in later years was diagnosed as schizophrenic. But none of us—including him—knew then he was mentally ill. When the hallucinations began, he'd drink to try and get relief."

Rosa's way of dealing with this pattern was to hole up in her room. She stayed there alone, trying to get rid of the terrifying thoughts and feelings her home life engendered. Usually she played her guitar or escaped into sleep.

When Rosa was fifteen, her mom—who had long abused her—got a divorce. Rosa's father was institutionalized. Rosa took the first step toward wholeness that same chaotic year. "I started reading one of those Bibles the Gideons give out. When I read the Gospel of John, the love I saw there astounded me. It was different from anything I'd ever been exposed to."

She told God that she hated her mom and dad and couldn't forgive them. She started going to church. But she was seen as just one of the teenagers and not someone who needed special help. That experience continued in every church she attended throughout her high school and young adult years. "No one knew I had problems or else they didn't know how to approach me."

But during a summer break at college, she spent a month at Francis and Edith Schaeffer's L'Abri community in Switzerland. "That's where I learned that it's okay to ask questions and expect a reasonable answer."

In 1977 she graduated from college, got married, and tried to establish a normal family life. But she didn't know what "normal" was. She was also belligerent and explosive due to the anger she'd stored up.

That year she began attending a house church and became a regular in one of their weekly small groups. "There, I had more personal contact with other Christians than I'd had in church before. Our little group of six or so studied Scripture and shared from our personal lives regularly. Once after a small group Bible study in which I'd been very argumentative, a member took me aside. 'There's something I need to tell you. I believe you're an angry person.' I cried."

But it was the beginning of her pursuit of help. She asked

a church leader if it was okay for a Christian to go for counseling. Assured that counseling was a good idea, she began seeing someone who came with Christian recommendations. For several years, she was in and out of counseling. But when she found herself taking out her pent-up rage on her little boy and her husband, she became frightened and went back for more intensive therapy.

As part of therapy, her counselor suggested she join an Adult Children of Alcoholics group, which she did. The more she heard others tell their stories, the more she began to recognize that being raised in an alcoholic, abusive home was the source of her problems. "I began to put two and two together: I was treated this way as a kid; that's why I think and act this way today." During support group meetings based on the Twelve Steps (see Appendix), she learned coping skills.

Finally, she began seeing her father, who had been released from the mental institution and had become a member of Alcoholics Anonymous. Today Rosa and her dad have been able to heal old wounds. "We don't even have to talk about the past any more."

People in her church accept and encourage her. She's grown close to some and as a result is continuing to replace wrong ideas about relationships with new, more healthy ones.

An Alcoholic Who Almost Died

Mary's first addiction was to over-the-counter sleeping pills. "I worked and worked to get myself off them," she says. Two weeks after she stopped taking them, she took her first drink.

"The first time I drank was at a party," recalls Mary. "I got so drunk that I blacked out." That became her pattern. Even though she drank three to five nights a week, it never occurred to her that she was an alcoholic.

Mary's guilt was enormous because she had been raised in a church and family that strongly disapproved of drinking. Consequently, she worked extra hard to keep her problem secret.

She knows now that she used alcohol to escape from the effects of a devastating childhood. "Mom was mentally ill and out of control much of the time. Both of my parents were mentally, emotionally, and sexually abusive." Her mother remained at home, her mental illness untreated.

The eldest of three children, Mary assumed the responsibility to do all she could to control her mother's violent outbursts as well as keep her father happy and under control emotionally. "The more I failed, the more I hated myself."

When she was twenty-one, Mary went to a leader in her church for help. Her father had died and she felt as though she was falling apart. But the church leader's response was, "You don't need counseling."

"When I found out that he wouldn't help me, I felt as though I was backed into a corner." Her church had a rigid code of conduct, and one thing the leadership definitely disapproved of was for members to go outside the church for counseling.

She dropped out of that church and tried to stop drinking on her own. But after a month of sobriety, Mary reasoned that it would be okay to drink again.

It didn't take long to fall into the old pattern. Since she lived alone, she had no family to point out her aberrant behavior. "But when I got drunk, my cat was terrified of me. I was so disgusted . . . that I was the kind of person a little animal would be afraid of."

In January of the next year, her life hit bottom. She became very ill with allergies she'd had since birth. One of the substances to which she was extremely allergic was alcohol. The stress of trying to be everything to everybody had taken its toll as well.

It was an acquaintance named Edna who stepped in to help. Even though the two had met only once, Edna awoke one night with the strong feeling that Mary was in trouble and began to pray for her. Then Edna woke her husband and told him, "I have to go get Mary."

Mary had gone to bed desperately ill and knowing she should get medical help, but she hadn't done it. The next morning, she could hardly walk.

When Edna came to the door, Mary had to use everything she had to get to it. Once it was open she fell into Edna's arms. Edna took her home and cared for her the next six months. During that time, Mary lost everything she had—from her home to her cat, which she couldn't keep because she was allergic to it.

Mary couldn't and didn't drink during those six months. And for four years after she left Edna's home, she couldn't work. But finally, with medical help, a very stringent diet, and plenty of fresh air and exercise, she started to get better while she carefully avoided alcohol.

When she made a trip to Mexico in 1984, however, the craving for alcohol returned. "My craving was so strong after years of abstinence, I realized I needed help." Prompted by two conversations—one with someone in Mexico who'd just started attending Alcoholics Anonymous, and a friend back home who'd started attending, too—Mary decided to go to AA herself.

"At the initial meeting, for the first time in my life I felt that I fit someplace. People cared about me." But it took ten months for Mary to admit that she was an alcoholic. Doing so was a turning point.

She hasn't had to fight the urge to drink since. She's also received counseling to help her deal with the effects of sexual abuse. Resolving those problems has also lessened her desire for alcohol. Meetings she attends of Adult Children of Alcoholics have helped her deal with behavior patterns formed early in life.

Recently, Mary began going to church again—not the one in which she was raised. In autumn 1989, she made a personal commitment to Jesus Christ.

Her new church's emphasis on God's grace has had a profound impact on her, for now she understands that He really does love her. She says it's great to experience that love through the Christians she's come to know.

Life with an Addicted Son

"For a year-and-a-half, we didn't know where our son Ted was," Ruth recalls. "Every time the police found a body, every time a store was held up, I'd read the description in a panic to see if it was him. If it wasn't for the Lord and his people, I don't know how I would have made it."

Ruth and Ken had adopted Ted as an infant. "He was a hyperactive child with an extremely short attention span," she recalls. "The older he got, the more erratic his behavior became." Ruth and Ken tried every treatment they could find, but the problem persisted.

It was during those years that the school district psychologist told Ruth that Ted's problems were the fault of Ruth and Ken, that they "weren't disciplining him enough." That statement would cause her to live with guilt for years.

Ted began drinking and smoking marijuana in his early teens. "He became violent when he drank. We have dents in the refrigerator, cracks in the sink, and patches in the kitchen wall from those outbursts." But information about substance abuse was scarce in those days, and it took Ruth a while to realize what really was his problem.

A year after Ted graduated from high school in 1982, Ruth and Ken felt it was dangerous to have the young man at home. Besides being violent, he stole from them and other family members. So they moved him out of the house.

Ted moved in and out again several times, until Ruth and Ken realized that taking him back only worsened his problems. The fact that Ruth and Ken agreed about their course of action was a lifesaver. "We had other serious family difficulties to deal with during those years. I don't think I could have handled differences between us on this."

Ruth didn't know it at the time, but that same year Ted was given a Gideon New Testament. He had filled in the page in the back that asks the reader to make a commitment to Jesus Christ. Ted didn't say anything to her, but later on Ruth found the New Testament among his things.

No one in her church ever made Ruth feel any less of a Christian because her child was an addict. Although church leaders weren't able to work with Ted because most of the time he lived elsewhere, Ruth remembers many important things they did to help her through. When others in the congregation admitted that they, too, were going through serious family problems as well, Ruth didn't feel like such an outsider. One family had a son in prison, and Ruth and they prayed for and supported one another. When things were especially bad, Ruth knew she could stop at the pastor's office after work and he'd pray with her.

Sometimes she felt guilty about monopolizing the prayer meeting and prayer chain with her requests. But then a woman told her, "That's what these support systems are all about."

Daily devotions helped, too. "Prayer has sustained me," she says.

During the year and a half when they didn't know where Ted was, Ruth and Ken would hear periodically from someone who'd seen him. But by the time they got the information, Ted had moved on.

The couple was on a trip when they ran into Ted on the street and the three of them talked for about ten minutes. "I call that 'my June miracle,'" says Ruth. "We were only in that area once a year." After that, the three of them kept in touch by phone.

One Saturday night about a year later, Ruth received an emergency phone call from a girl in a bar in another part of the state. Ted was there; he was suicidal and close to convulsions. The caller said Ted was ready for treatment.

In the space of a few hours, Ruth and Ken raced to where Ted was, lined up a treatment center, scraped together $3,000 cash to get him in, and transported him to the center —all without having had any previous experience in how to do such things.

Ted stayed for the thirty-one-day treatment. His parents spent countless hours driving back and forth to the center, seeing Ted and attending meetings.

After release, Ted did well for a while. But he drifted back to old friends and old addictions. "Once you get back on it, you pick up where you left off and go downhill fast," says Ruth. Ted requested help again, but after two weeks the rehab center put him out because he wasn't willing to make a life change. Before a year was up, he was homeless and shooting heroin.

Finally, he checked himself into a Salvation Army center where he entered a treatment program. He stayed with the Salvation Army about a year. He was released over a year ago and at this writing is still straight and clean.

In the meantime, Ruth has learned everything she can about addiction and has attended Al-Anon meetings (for families of alcoholics). But she credits an addictionologist, a specialist in addiction, with being the professional who helped most. "From him I've understood what my responsibilities are and are not with Ted. He's the one who helped me get rid of the load of guilt I'd been carrying."

Still, she has to commit her son's future to God and live her life one day at a time—the same way her son has to live his.

Keep Dan in mind when you counsel a substance-abusing teenager; you'll be better able to understand the double life he's living and its consequences. When you talk with the adult child of an alcoholic, let Rosa's story remind you how confused such a victim can become and how much long-term help and encouragement he or she will need.

Remembering Mary can prompt you to persevere because, without help, the addict's condition will deteriorate and he or she may even die. Ruth typifies family members of abusers in your church. What helped her is likely to help them. Keep in mind, too, what some of these people did *not* have: an informed, caring, confrontive Christian in their lives when they needed one. The following chapters will show you how to *be* that person.

CHAPTER THREE

COUNSELING THE ADDICT

W HAT IS YOUR ROLE AS A PASTOR, YOUTH LEADER, or other Christian helper in counseling the substance abuser?

You can:

• Guide the addict to face the fact that he or she has a problem;

• Help the person submit to God for help in gaining wholeness and a new life;

• See that he or she enters appropriate treatment;

• Support the person through the struggle to recovery.

How much you can accomplish will vary from case to case. In any event, the user does need a caring individual outside the family who knows how the addict's mind works and what are the most effective ways to intervene. Left alone, the addict is likely to keep abusing substances, perhaps losing everything that was once important.

Though you may have limited experience dealing with substance abusers, you needn't feel helpless. First of all, your job isn't to "cure" them. It *is* to come alongside and guide them toward the most appropriate treatment, which will usually be provided by a professional. The counseling outlines in this book will show you how to do that guiding.

Second, you have what's most important: genuine concern, willingness, and the Holy Spirit to give insight.

Assessing Your Role

The guidelines given in this chapter presuppose that you have general training and experience in counseling. We assume you know how to make the counselee comfortable, draw him or her out, reflect back what he or she has said, and employ other basic skills.

Unfortunately, most pastors and youth leaders have had little or no specific training in long-term work with addicts —and that's what's needed. A basic rule to follow is not to go any farther than your expertise allows. Know when it's time to refer to trained professionals. That includes times when you find yourself not making any headway after repeated attempts to help. It becomes evident that the counselee isn't cooperating so that his or her life will change. If the addict is physically or sexually abusing a family member, you also need to refer him or her to a trained professional. Refer if the addict poses a danger to himself, herself, or to others. Other times to refer are described in this chapter.

More Than Clean and Sober

Experienced, long-term help is also needed because the individual has to do more than just stop using drugs and/or alcohol. That only produces a "dry" alcoholic or addict— someone who may be clean and sober but hasn't dealt with the problems that led him or her to abuse substances in the first place. If the root causes are not addressed, it is only a matter of time before the person returns to abusing substances or to some other equally detrimental behavior.

If, for example, the addict drinks to forget feelings of anxiety or depression, he or she needs to discover the source of those feelings and learn how to change them or cope with them in more appropriate ways. There may also be a physical, mental, or emotional illness that needs treatment.

A 58-year-old Northwestern businessman, for example, stopped drinking several years ago. He insisted on doing it "on my own," without therapy or support group. While remaining sober, he still lives behind an emotional wall that keeps him from real communication with his family.

Warning

When dealing with an addict, it's critical to remember not to simply recommend flushing the pills down the toilet or stopping use of the substance "cold turkey." While some drugs aren't dangerous to stop without medical help, others are.

In the case of barbiturates, for example, the person could die of respiratory arrest in twenty-four hours unless withdrawal is done gradually.

Detoxification from severe alcohol abuse is dangerous as well. The person may initially go through withdrawal and feel good, but delirium tremens can set in two weeks after he or she is dry. In such a case the individual could have a seizure behind the wheel of a car, with devastating consequences. Detoxification under the supervision of a medical professional is necessary.

Counseling an Adult

How might you encounter a substance abuser? There are at least three possibilities:

1. The abuser seeks you out. Generally secretive about his or her problem—particularly around disapproving acquaintances—the abuser will probably come only when in desperation. It may be because she's just narrowly escaped injury to herself and others while driving under the influence. Or perhaps he's been given an ultimatum by his spouse: "Get help or get out!"

The addict may come for a reason seemingly unrelated to addiction. Jean brought her sixteen-year-old son "because he's out of control. He's out all hours with kids I don't trust." You realize that her son's rebellion has a reason, and wonder if there's a problem in the home. One possibility could be parental substance abuse.

2. *You initiate a meeting.* A church member's behavior has changed; perhaps there are symptoms of drug or alcohol use listed in Chapter 1. Or the person may be withdrawn, absent from church, not acting responsibly, or showing signs of trouble in family life.

3. *A church member lets you know he or she suspects a problem.* Darlene confides that Jane, who's in her small group Bible study, is worried sick because her husband is using drugs and may be selling them as well.

The Approach

Make the person comfortable. If he or she readily admits a substance abuse problem, draw the person out until you think you have a pretty accurate picture.

If he or she comes to you for another reason, don't accuse the person of addiction. Instead, direct the conversation so it will be natural for the person to admit it himself or herself. The following is an example of questions you might ask.

Jean brings her sixteen-year-old daughter to you because the girl is rebellious and stays out late. *Always give your attention to the person who comes as counselee—in this case, the daughter.*

Helper (to daughter): "Your mother says you just won't listen. What do you think the problem is?"

Daughter: "I hate being at home."

Helper (reflecting and enlarging on her remarks): "Being home is hard for you. What about it is hard?"

Daughter: "Mom's always on me about something."

Helper: "What's going on with Mom that makes her argue with you?

You would try to bring the daughter to the place where it's finally natural for her to tell you, "Mom drinks too much." You could then talk to the parent about her underlying problem with alcohol and say that it needs to be addressed *along with* the daughter's rebelliousness.

If you're initiating the meeting, you might say something like, "I've missed you at the men's prayer fellowship, Bob. You seem distant lately, too. Have there been changes in your life—something you might want to talk about? I really do care about you."

You may go on to suggest that the two of you get together to talk. When the meeting takes place, draw him out. If you extend nonjudgmental trust, he may eventually tell you his real problem.

The Assessment

One way to get information about a person's drug or alcohol use is to ask about the stresses in his or her life. That includes physical problems, the person's emotional state, how well he or she has been sleeping, etc. During the process, you can ask, "How much alcohol do you consume? What kind? What kind of drugs do you take?" If a medical checkup is indicated, be sure to recommend one.

Getting an Evaluation

As you counsel, keep in mind that there are two kinds of addiction. The first is psychological (known as *habituation*) in which the person becomes dependent on a substance as a source of pleasure, escape, or reassurance. The second is physiological—the dependence of the body on certain substances. Telling the difference between these two types of addiction is just one job of the experts.

If, in your conversation, evidence of substance abuse is revealed, urge the individual to agree to an evaluation at a local rehabilitation center. You can arrange to meet with the person after the assessment so you can help him or her take the next step.

Explain: "A person at the center will give you a test to find out if you have a problem—and if so, what kind and how serious it is. If necessary, they'll recommend treatment."

Often these assessments are free. Before recommending a rehabilitation center, check with trustworthy Christian counselors, doctors, and pastors in your area to determine which centers have a good track record. Then offer to go with the individual if he or she wishes.

Reaching Out to God

As early in the counseling process as possible, the counselee needs to acknowledge his or her addiction and reach out to God for help. Michael may finally admit, "I'm into crack, and it's got me hooked. It's ruining my life, and I can't go on this way."

That may be the time to follow up with, "God is ready and willing to help you overcome this addiction. Reach out to Him." If and when the person is ready, lead in a prayer of surrender to God.

Counseling the person to surrender to God needs to take place as early as possible in the recovery process. However, the counselee may not be ready to do that during your initial conversation because of denial that the problem exists. Or if the problem is acknowledged, the person may believe self-treatment can handle it.

Be sensitive to the counselee's mindset. The opportunity to present God as the true source of help may come when the person is in treatment and/or in a Twelve Step program that emphasizes submission to a "Higher Power." Then you can reinforce what is learned by defining who God is as described in the Bible and what kind of relationship the person can have with Him. Always provide the counselee with spiritual truth so he or she has a foundation for trust. In future sessions, you can teach more about life in fellowship with God.

You'll also want to introduce him or her to Jesus Christ if he or she doesn't know the Lord as Savior. As with other spiritual counseling, remain sensitive in your timing. More specific principles for leading an addict to Christ and other spiritual counseling guidelines are described in Chapter 4.

Recognizing Denial

Often the abuser refuses to admit he or she has a problem. This roadblock is called "denial." The person is filtering out the facts he or she doesn't want to face. For example, if the person is experiencing blackouts—which are chemically-induced amnesia—he or she may say, "I just fall asleep."

When confronted with his or her drinking, an abuser's response might be, "I can handle it." Here are other examples of denial statements you may hear:

• "Sure, I take sleeping pills occasionally, but it's no big deal."

• "I may have a beer or so to help me relax after work, that's all."

• "Just about all the kids I know smoke some pot, but that doesn't make them drug addicts."

Expect the counselee to use distorted logic. Instead of seeing drinking or drug use as the primary problem, he or she will reverse the order: "I use it because of my problems."

Intervention: One Answer to Denial

How to break through denial? The most successful way is for the helper to initiate what's called "an intervention." Developed within the last fifteen years, it's a meeting organized and led by a professional (called an "interventionist") that's attended by family members, close friends, and the addict.

Its purpose is for loved ones, each in turn, to tell the addict through story after story how the habit has caused them pain. In this way they create a crisis designed to shatter the addict's defenses instead of waiting for serious health problems, job loss, or trouble with the law to do that.

Confrontation of the addict's offense is Scriptural. Jesus provided a model in Matthew 18:15-17:
- Go to the sinner individually.
- If he or she won't listen, take one or two others along.
- If he or she still denies the problem, tell it to the church.

(Church discipline as a last resort is discussed in Chapter 8.)

It's time to recommend intervention when key family members and/or those close to the addict admit there's a problem even though the addict doesn't, and are ready to do what it takes to help.

Describe to key people in the addict's life what intervention is. You'll want to explain that over ninety percent of all interventions lead the addict into treatment. If you are close to the addict, you can volunteer to be on the team.

Explain that an intervention team consists of from three to eight people. Usually it's the spouse who initiates intervention, but anyone close to the individual can do so. Point out that it's more loving to confront the addict than to allow the person to destroy himself or herself.

Describe the intervention process itself. Explain that each person who is to make a statement to the addict will meet with the interventionist first (without the addict present) to learn facts about addiction, rehearse what he or she will say, and prepare for the meeting. Participants may write out what they plan to say to the addict.

A daughter might write, "Last week at the school play, you showed up drunk. You were so loud that everyone was looking at you. I was really embarrassed and worried about you."

A spouse might write, "The first of the month you went in my wallet and took the money I was going to use to make the house payment. You spent it on drinks for you and your friends. I felt hurt and betrayed that alcohol meant more to you than the well-being of your family."

At the intervention, the professional will say something

39

like this to the addict: "Your family and friends have gathered out of love for you and have things they'd like to say." Each team member will read or say what he or she has rehearsed.

Assure loved ones and friends that they needn't fear that the addict will get out of control and perhaps even become violent. It's the interventionist's job to deal with emotional outbursts. The interventionist will assure the addict that after everyone has a chance to speak, he or she will have a chance to respond.

If they're open to the idea, help family members locate a good interventionist. These experts often work out of local treatment centers. Get recommendations from Christian counselors, doctors, or other pastors. Be sure the family finds out the interventionist's fee. Know what kind of certification or licensing is required in your state and whether those on your list are properly accredited.

Seven years ago, Sandi (whose story was told in Chapter 1) read about intervention and contacted an interventionist well-known in her area. The whole family gathered at his office to plan a confrontation with Sandi's dad. After learning about addiction and the format of an intervention meeting, each wrote a statement to be read to Sandi's dad, focusing on the damage substance abuse had caused.

Sandi recalls that she was very nervous. "I asked myself what was the worst thing that could happen. We'd lose our father's physical presence. Wasn't that better than having him die from alcoholism?"

At the beginning of the intervention meeting, Sandi's dad was angry. When Sandi's turn came, she began, "Dad, I'm here because I love you." After each family member had spoken, her dad said, "I never thought I was an alcoholic. Now I know that I am."

Let family members know that before the intervention takes place, they'll need to make a reservation at a treatment center. In that way, the addict can enter immediately after the confrontation is over.

An Overview of the Recovery Process

Whether the addict confronts his or her problem during a crisis or through intervention, substance abusers generally need detoxification, therapy, and some kind of support.

Detoxification takes place in a treatment center or can be done under the direction of a physician. Therapy begins either in the treatment center or with private counseling and needs to continue afterward for as long as necessary. Support can take place through a Twelve Step group or may be provided through church groups.

Dan, whose story is told in Chapter 2, agreed to go to a treatment center for an evaluation. "I thought I could con my way through that, too," he says. "I knew all the answers." When he got there, he discovered that his physician had preadmitted him. "I was angry. I felt as though I wasn't worth the time and money." The treatment did lead to Dan's recovery, however.

Choosing a Treatment Center

A Christian-oriented treatment center is preferable because it uses biblical principles. An alternative would be a secular center with key staff people who are Christians. If neither is available, advise the family to select a reputable secular center, but always avoid treatment that promises a quick cure. When beginning sobriety has been achieved, the person can build a spiritual base. Guidelines are provided in Chapter 4.

A good center works with each family member, identifying that person's role in the dysfunction, exploring wounds caused by addiction, and encouraging personal growth necessary for everyone's recovery. The center should combine participation for every member in some kind of support group, some insight-oriented therapy and/or behavioral therapy, and set reachable goals. Random urinalysis of the addict to screen for substance use should be part of the routine.

Find out what the qualifications for staff people are. In times past, centers tended to hire those who were addicts but were now clean and sober themselves. However, most did not have much training. Fortunately, more centers now require professional training.

Centers offer two kinds of treatment: inpatient and outpatient. Advise inpatient treatment if any of the following is true.

1. The addict has a long history of addiction.

2. He or she is experiencing medical complications or deterioration due to substance abuse.

3. He or she has completed outpatient treatment but has relapsed.

4. The addict is living in an environment that supports continued substance use.

5. He or she needs the structure and security of inpatient programming.

Inpatient treatment requires the patient to live in the facility an average of thirty days (it may be longer or shorter), away from family and job. Such treatment has a medical component that includes nutrition and exercise.

In outpatient treatment, the person comes for therapy for perhaps five nights a week at first, and then decreases attendance gradually. Outpatient treatment allows the addict to maintain a work schedule while attending sessions.

When There Is No Money or Insurance

Let the family know that centers operated by state agencies are usually geared for indigent to middle-income people. Even private centers that receive public funds must make some beds available for low-income people, indigents, and welfare recipients. Check local laws.

Usually there is a waiting list and the addict must call daily or weekly to maintain his or her place on that list. While you can put the addict in touch with such centers, under most circumstances it's not a good idea to do the calling for him or her. If the addict must wait to get into a center and his or her condition requires it, make arrangements to go to a hospital or other facility for detoxification, which takes from two to five days. The person's physician may be able to recommend such a place. When the addict is released, put him or her in contact with an appropriate substance abuse support group (like AA) until he or she can get into a treatment center and begin the program.

Counseling Youth

There may be more opportunities to help teenagers who are using drugs and/or alcohol than there are to help adults. Youth workers are more likely to get close to kids and observe them. In addition, other kids often know who's doing what, and word is likely to get back to the youth worker.

Youth certainly need our attention in this area. The average alcohol abuser was twelve and a half years old when he or she began to drink. At least two million of the alcoholics in the United States are teenagers. Alcoholism develops more rapidly in adolescents because they metabolize alcohol more quickly than adults do.

Youth tend to experiment with both drugs and alcohol. One recent survey showed that about ninety percent of older teenagers have tried alcohol and forty percent have tried marijuana. Figures also show that the number of youth who think it's okay to try marijuana, cocaine, and alcohol jumped during the years 1977-1988. There are also more "polyusers" (users of more than one substance) than ever. The longer they use, the harder they are to treat. So it's urgent to get to them early.

Spotting a Problem

Symptoms of substance abuse include mood swings, a change in peer group, weight loss and other physical deterioration, becoming argumentative, disappearing from home, skipping school, and missing items (such as stereos that can be sold for drug money). Watch for kids who are dropping out of church activities. See Chapter 1 for other signs. Of course, for some young people these symptoms can be typical of adolescence—mood swings, arguments as the teenager tries to establish autonomy, and dropping out of church activities for the same reason—so avoid making unfounded accusations. But be alert and take the following steps when they are warranted.

Steps to Take

1. Initiate a conversation with the young person if you suspect substance use. Express your concern and mention the behavioral changes you have observed and anything else that is pertinent. Then give the young person time to talk.

Most commonly the teenager will deny use or, if confronted with irrefutable evidence, will answer with something like Dan did in Chapter 2: "It's the first time, and I didn't get high."

2. Contact the parents or guardian and arrange for all of you—including the young person—to talk about the situation openly. Be prepared, however, for parental resistance also. Often parents are the ones in whom denial is strongest. Even physicians whose sons or daughters have behavior problems sometimes have no idea drugs and/or alcohol are involved.

Tricia's mother, a nurse, is one example. Tired of her sixteen-year-old daughter's failing grades and defiant behavior, the woman took the girl to a counselor. "Even though I was a trained medical professional, even though I'd found marijuana among her possessions (which she denied was hers), I refused to admit that using drugs could be the reason she'd changed. I simply couldn't face facts. I feel terrible when I think of the time I wasted denying the truth, in the face of the fact that she was showing obvious signs of marijuana use."

3. Try to get the adolsecent to go for treatment voluntarily. It may be private counseling with someone experienced in treating young substance abusers. The teenager might also attend a substance abuse support group. If necessary, suggest an evaluation at a treatment center.

It may be a good idea to have another mature Christian outside the family talk with the adolescent about treatment. Choose someone close to him or her, like a youth leader, a teacher, or a club leader.

4. If the situation warrants it and the young person refuses to cooperate, advise the parents to take him or her for a surprise urinalysis to detect the presence of chemicals. It may not show the presence of alcohol, but it lets the teenager know that the parent is definitely on top of things.

How does a surprise urinalysis work? Once in a treatment center, an attendant will go into the bathroom with the young person and observe collection of the specimen. If the adolescent refuses to cooperate, the family can ask the attendant to say something like, "I'll stay here as long as I need to until the job is done." If the teenager absolutely refuses, a blood test can be taken and will achieve the same results. When those results are known, a conversation about treatment with the specialists can follow.

5. Only if this fails to bring the teen to treatment should the parents search the youth's room for alcohol, drugs, and paraphernalia. This will create an emotional scene in an already emotionally-charged situation.

6. At this point, the helper may suggest that the family arrange for an intervention.

7. If the young person's life is growing more and more

out of control and treatment continues to be refused, recommend that the parents take him or her for treatment anyway. They may say something like, "I'm your parent, and I've decided that you're going to get help." The adults involved simply can't wait for a fifteen or sixteen year old to decide what's best. Chances are that no one will break through the teen's denial until after he or she is in treatment.

8. Strongly encourage the rest of the family to go into treatment, too. That means participating in the programs at a treatment center and taking part in private family counseling. Family members may also attend a support group.

9. If parents refuse to investigate the problem, you can pray that they'll change their minds. Sometimes that only happens if the youth gets arrested or flunks out of school.

10. Be ready to talk with the young person about God. As with adults, you'll need the Holy Spirit's guidance to know when the person is open to Him. Share the same information as with adults: who God is, His desire to help, the salvation He offers, and how to become a mature Christian.

If you have concrete evidence of drug use or of a minor in possession of alcohol, you can report it to the police. When making that decision, keep in mind that the individual could drive under the influence and harm himself or herself and/or someone else—even fatally. You could prevent a tragedy.

The Need for Time

Unless God chooses to perform a miracle, there are no quick cures for addiction—no matter what the addict's age. Be positive with both addict and family because they have taken a constructive first step and are acquiring the knowledge and skills necessary for recovery; but don't raise false hopes for an instant solution.

Falling back into the habit is common. If Burt smokes

marijuana because he lost a big sale after two months of being clean, or if parents discover that Heather has been skipping support group meetings and is hiding beer in the closet just a few weeks out of treatment, be realistic. Help the addict forgive himself or herself; help family members to forgive him or her, too. Urge the person to learn from his or her fall by finding constructive ways to deal with the temptation next time. Show the person that he or she needs to keep "working the steps" that bring recovery—which includes depending on God. (For a fuller discussion of working the steps, see the question and answer on this subject in Chapter 8.)

When an addict falls, he or she may need more counseling or, in some cases, may need to go through rehabilitation again. Approximately one-half of those receiving treatment at a rehab center have to repeat it. Always emphasize the philosophy that Alcoholics Anonymous has made famous: "Live one day at a time."

No matter how hard you try, not every addict will face his or her problem, go into therapy, or see it through to recovery. That doesn't mean the work you do is wasted. Seeds have been planted, and in answer to prayer God can work in the person's life. At another time, when the crisis is severe enough, the person may have a change of heart.

CHAPTER FOUR

SCRIPTURE, ADDICTION, AND SPIRITUAL FREEDOM

SINCE SCRIPTURE IS THE CHRISTIAN'S ULTIMATE AUTHORity for faith and practice, you'll need an understanding of its teaching on the use of drugs and alcohol. This chapter will explore what the Bible has to say about key issues on the subject. It will also provide a counseling model to restore the addict to fellowship with God.

Most of the Scriptures quoted in this chapter refer specifically to alcoholic beverages. Keep in mind that alcohol is a drug—a mind-altering substance with the potential for physical or psychological addiction in some people. The fact that our society classifies it differently is more a matter of cultural convention than of clear, scientific logic. So it is reasonable to extend the application of Scriptural warnings about alcohol to the use of other drugs.

A Gift of God?

The use of wine is linked with blessings from God in both the Old and New Testaments. Isaac prayed for "an abundance of grain and new wine" for his son, Jacob (Gen. 27:28). Moses included new wine as one of the symbols of God's blessing to the new nation, Israel. Wine was served at the wedding where Jesus' first miracle is recorded.

Wine was also used in temple sacrifices as a drink offering to God and as a temple tithe. Many times it was included in lists of produce indicating it was part of the typical diet. So, at the very least, it was considered to be of some value both by the Jews and God (Lev. 23:13 and Deut. 14:23).

But even a gift from God can be abused. Nabal, whose

name means "foolish," is a biblical example of the many who have abused alcohol with devastating consequence. He became so intoxicated that he couldn't tend to business or communicate with his wife. When he did sober up and his wife told him about the battle she had averted, "his heart failed him" (I Sam. 25:37). About ten days later, he was dead. When Elah, King of Israel, got drunk, Zimri came in and killed him, usurping the throne (I Kings 16:9). King Ahab of Israel routed Ben-Hadad and thirty-two other kings while they got drunk in their tent, making plans to attack Israel (I Kings 20:15-21). Paul couldn't have been more accurate when he said, "Do not get drunk on wine, which leads to debauchery" (Eph. 5:18).

Opinions differ as to whether Christians should use alcohol at all, but everyone agrees that drunkenness is prohibited. And there are few differences of opinion when it comes to the use of illegal drugs. In contrast to such things as wine and beer, drugs have no food value at all. Some commonly abused drugs are valuable for medicinal purposes when used as directed (by a physician if prescribed, or by label instructions if over-the-counter). In that sense, they, too, are God's gift. But their use for *any* other purpose or under any other circumstance is abuse—both detrimental and dangerous.

The person who comes from a home where drugs or alcohol have been abused should avoid these substances altogether. Research seems to suggest these people are at high risk for addiction. The addict must totally avoid them as well.

Spiritually Counseling the Addict

As was pointed out in Chapter 3, it is vital to introduce the abuser to the God of the Bible and to His Son. The time to do so varies with the situation.

Of course, one doesn't have to be a Christian to become

49

drug- and alcohol-free. Countless nonreligious people have done so. Yet, most effective addict support groups emphasize the need to depend on a "Higher Power" to become whole.

Furthermore, the person who knows Christ personally has been spiritually reborn. He or she can know the Holy Spirit as strength, guide, and teacher. The individual has a freedom found nowhere else, and an eternal purpose for living.

Be careful, though, how and with whom you use Scripture. Some addicts may interpret it in a way that's helpful. But others, because of their depressed condition, will find judgment in even the most uplifting passages. Until they're able to grasp God's true meaning, you may want to use Scriptural principles without identifying the source. In that way the information is less threatening but still becomes part of the person's thinking process.

For example, you might tell Christine, who's addicted to drugs and depressed: "In his Word, God promises to forgive you. Here's what He says: 'If we confess our sins, he is faithful and just and will forgive us our sins and purify us from all unrighteousness.'"

Christine: "But I can't confess all my sins. I don't even *know* all my sins."

Though you try to convince her that she can confess what she does know, she remains unconvinced. For some counselees, love, forgiveness, and acceptance will have to be demonstrated in person and later connected to Scripture. Then the counselee will be better able to believe because he or she has experienced living examples.

In counseling, focus on the key issue: The person needs to believe that God is sufficient and can be trusted to help conduct his or her daily affairs. Instead of doing that, the addict has been looking for other ways to meet his or her need. The more the person turns to a substance instead of to God, the more he or she avoids repentance and trust.

Eventually, his or her heart becomes hardened, a condition Paul warns against in Hebrews 3:8, 15.

Explain What God Says about Substance Abuse

Be sensitive to the Holy Spirit's leading. Your goal is to help the person see addiction from a biblical perspective, not to make him or her feel like a terrible person.

• *Addiction is forbidden* (Rom. 13:13; I Cor. 5:11; 6:10; Eph. 5:18; and I Pet. 4:3).

• *A drunkard is described as one who is out of control* (Isa. 19:14).

• *Substance abuse is identified with rebelliousness against authority* (Deut. 21:20).

• *The abuser is disobeying Scripture when the substances used are illegal* (Rom. 13:1, 2).

• *Leaders are warned against alcohol use*, which shows its inherent danger. Priests, before entering the tabernacle (Lev. 10:9), kings, and other rulers also were to stay away from these substances (Prov. 31:4, 5). Elders, deacons, and mature women—probably responsible for instruction of the young—are disqualified from service if they are addicted to wine (I Tim. 3:3, 8; Titus 1:7; 2:3).

• *The ultimate end of the addict is destruction* (Hos. 4:11; Isa. 28:1; Prov. 23:21).

For the addict, his or her substance of choice becomes an idol; the addict *lives* to obtain and use it. It is a self-centered way of living, as Paul points out when he warns those getting drunk at the Lord's table and ignoring others in the congregation (I Cor. 11:21). Paul characterizes this behavior as opposite to that which reflects the spirit of Christ and His sacrifice for the needs of others.

Theologian Richard Mouw states that for him, Romans 1 "is the central biblical passage for understanding a 'theology of addiction'. . . . We rebel against God and suppress the truth in unrighteousness and . . . are then 'given over' to it."[1]

51

A former addict recalls how it was for him. "Before I went to work, I smoked a joint. On my way there, I'd stop off and have a couple of beers and buy enough to get me through the work day. All day, I'd be thinking about getting home so I could use as much as I wanted. Using was what I lived for. It had priority over family—everything."

As you counsel an addict, it is important to show that sin is universal. Don't give the counselee the idea that you're saying, "Addicts are terrible!" Point out that the same list of sins that condemns drunkenness also includes such character flaws as envying and covetousness. (See Rom. 13:8-13 and I Cor. 6:9, 10.)

Neither the helper nor anyone else in the addict's life dares adopt a pharisaical attitude. Keep reminding yourself and others that, while our sin may not be as obvious as that of our addicted brother or sister, it is also grievous to God. We have no ground to adopt an "us" and "them" attitude.

Leading the Addict to Christ

God's attitude toward the addict is no different from His attitude toward anyone else. He loves *every* sinner; Jesus Christ came to seek and save *all* the lost.

Before you present the plan of salvation, be sure the person is able to think clearly. If drugs and/or alcohol have clouded and distorted his or her mental processes, the person will be unable to make a rational decision to invite Christ into his or her life.

Make it clear that Christianity is not an easy answer to the person's problem. Many users have given assent to the ABC's of salvation with super optimism, but trashed the idea when it didn't provide instant relief.

Explain repentance carefully because the person may have lived in denial so long that he or she is out of touch with his or her sin and the need to be cleansed. Emphasize the fact that there's absolutely nothing the person can do to save himself or herself, but that Christ has done it all.

The addict needs Jesus Christ, not simply because he or she is an addict, but because every person has a sinful nature. God has provided the way of escape from the slavery of sin through the sacrifice of Jesus Christ (Rom. 8:1-4). The only requirement for this salvation is an acknowledgement of personal need and a willingness to believe in the sufficiency of Christ's sacrifice to meet that need as described in John 3:16.

Traditional salvation Scriptures can have particular meaning in these cases. Beneath his or her denial, the addict usually knows he or she has sinned and come short of God's glory (Rom. 3:23). The news that God actually offers eternal life through Christ as a gift (Rom. 6:23) can be overwhelming. But the simple offer to be saved from the penalty and power of sin by faith has been accepted by countless addicts who have begun new lives.

Forgiveness

Manuel, raised in a slum, became addicted to drugs as a young teenager. Soon he was selling, too. He came to see his life as useless and his future as non-existent.

In desperation, he began going to church and one Sunday went to the altar to pray for help. "I didn't know how to approach God and no one seemed to know how to help someone like me," he recalls.

Two years later, Manuel was sent to prison. When a minister began visiting him, Manuel was cynical. "You a do-gooder? Forget it. You can't help me. I tried God. It didn't work."

Patiently over the next few months, the pastor kept explaining, "God loves you. He wants to become part of your life—to forgive you, make you clean and come to live in you. By now you know you can't change yourself. God can. He wants to."

Manuel recalls: "Finally one day I took the step and received Christ." With careful discipleship, Manuel grew stronger. Today he's out of prison and helping people in the very city slums where he once lived as an addict.

The addict may receive Christ or may have done so in the past, but still needs to be taken slowly through the process of confession, forgiveness, and cleansing. It's outlined in I John 1:9: "If we confess our sins, he is faithful and just and will forgive us our sins and purify us from all unrighteousness." Doing so will probably require a series of sessions in which you'll go through the following stages.

Stage one. "I've lost control of my life." Review the fact that the person has become enslaved to a pattern of behavior in which the desire to be intoxicated or stoned has priority over everything else. Thinking it through, the person may say, "I spent money that should have gone to the kids," or "I got kicked off the team because I was too out of it."

After the person sees that salvation from the addiction is beyond his or her control, go on to show that God can save the person from himself or herself. If the person once tried trusting Christ for salvation, he or she will need to learn to trust Him day by day for the power to overcome the habit.

Keep reminding yourself that the addict may feel like an outcast and may need to be reassured that Jesus Himself was scorned for associating with sinners. Jesus rebuked His critics by reminding them that God wants to extend mercy.

For Skip, forgiveness seemed out of the question. Addicted to drugs, he told his wife, "It's better if I leave. Some people are good and some are bad. I'm one of the bad ones." He honestly believed that was true.

Instead, his wife insisted they get counseling. After listening to them, the pastor asked Skip to read I John 1:9. He did so. "After I read it," Skip recalls, "The pastor asked me to read it again. Then a third time. That's when it hit me. It said, 'and to cleanse us from all unrighteousness.' I didn't realize I could be forgiven. I'd acquired a pile of sins and thought there was no room for me in God's life."

Stage two. Help the addict face his or her pattern of denial, recognize it as destructive, and continue to ask God to remove it. Then help the person recount specific actions or thoughts that have supported the habit and hurt others.

Jill confesses, "I kept telling my husband that if he made more money, I wouldn't be under so much stress and have to take pills." Alice says, "I blamed my parents for being so religious and strict with me." You can ask the addict to write the thoughts and actions in a journal. As the addict recognizes these patterns as destructive, he or she must continue to ask God to remove them.

As the person becomes more willing to recognize the behavior as destructive, he or she is better able to choose alternatives that are more in line with God's will. Repentance is empowered by the Holy Spirit in response to genuine confession and the seeking of God's help.

Stage three. The addict makes a full confession of wrongs to those affected and attempts to make restitution wherever possible. In this way, he or she may be able to rebuild relationship bridges. The person also needs to be taught to keep short accounts as a way of life—that is, seek reconciliation quickly whenever new offenses occur.

Keith, a mature Christian, was taking 19-year-old Sam through the forgiveness process. "I've hurt so many people!" Sam kept repeating.

"Who have you hurt most?"

"My parents."

"How?"

"I lied to them, verbally abused them, refused to cooperate when they tried to help."

Together, Keith and Sam decided that the thing to do was to visit Sam's parents, apologize for specific wrongs, and ask their forgiveness.

"I also stole money—from my own grandmother. Can you imagine? I talked other kids into using drugs . . ."

Over time and with Keith's help, Sam decided what steps, if any, he could take in each situation that came to mind. Confessing to his parents, returning the money to his grandmother, and asking their forgiveness helped draw the family closer. Sam had to accept the fact that he couldn't "fix" everything in his past. But every positive action he could and did take made him feel cleaner.

At the same time that you're guiding the addict through the process of confession, it's important that he or she is also involved in a discipling program that encourages devotion to God. Central to this is familiarity with the Scripture and the development of a life of prayer.

You may choose to have him or her do a series of Bible studies, go through a particular book on the subject of discipleship that your church uses, and discuss with you or another capable Christian what is learned.

Often, it's prayer—that immediate contact with God—that will rescue the addict in a moment of temptation. Such a prayer should include two basic elements: confession that the person is under temptation, and a request for strength to deal with it. It may sound something like this: "God, I want a drink so bad. I am weak and just don't have what it takes to deal with this. Please help me. I surrender this temptation to you. Provide me with the strength to walk away from it. I know that part is my responsibility. Thank you, Lord."

Cultivating the ability to let God search his or her life is a survival skill the person desperately needs. Go over key points about prayer, pray together, rehearse ways to pray when under temptation, and invite the individual to participate in a small prayer group.

Stage four. Encourage the counselee to express his or her faith publicly to help solidify it. Direct the person to opportunities in which he or she will move out of self-concern and into empathetic concern for others. That may be by participating in a substance abuse support group and encouraging others just coming into treatment, or speaking to youth about addiction. Doing so reinforces the person's sense of values, shoring up an often deficient self-image. Paul put it this way: "Each of you should look not only to your own interests, but also to the interests of others" (Phil. 2:4).

CHAPTER FIVE

THE ADDICTED FAMILY

T HE FIRST THING TO KEEP IN MIND WHEN YOU MEET A close relative of an addict is that living with someone who's chemically dependent is just plain miserable. Spouses of addicts, their children, and parents need your help just as badly as does the substance abuser.

Codependency

A family member's misery results partially from experiencing the continual uncertainty of how that person will be from day to day—how uncaring, argumentative, or abusive. The whole family's focus is on the addict. As a result, family members become what is known as "codependent." This does not mean that they, too, are dependent on the substance as is the addict. Rather, they have had to organize their lives, beliefs, actions, values, and decisions around someone else—sometimes staying out of the addict's way, sometimes caring for the person, sometimes making excuses for him or her, sometimes denying that the addict has a problem—but always having their lives determined by that of the addict.

For example, a wife becomes completely preoccupied with her husband's drinking; her role as his nurse becomes her primary identity. "Through living with an alcoholic over a period of years, I became as sick mentally, physically, and spiritually as he," a wife said.[1]

A child may count on the hope that if she does everything right, her father will stop using drugs. Trying to please becomes her pattern for living, and she continues to behave that way when she grows up.

Family Deterioration

The second thing to keep in mind is that the family feels helplessly tied to the chemically dependent relative and goes through a destructive cycle. First, there is embarrassment; later, feelings of neglect, anxiety over the financial drain, loss of control, and anger and hurt masked by overwhelming concern.

In addition, family members are living double lives. To outsiders they may be seen as committed to one another. At home, they feel trapped. They may feel chained to an impossible situation. More aggressive family members may walk out and slam the door. Unfortunately, they take with them the unhealthy living patterns they have formed.

Counseling the Spouse

Generally, husbands and wives deny that substance abuse is *the* problem as much as the addict himself or herself does. A wife may come for help because she's feeling guilty—she just can't make her marriage work. Or she may be mentally and emotionally exhausted from trying to carry her husband's load, too.

A more confrontive woman like Karen, who discovered not long after her marriage that her husband was an alcoholic, may come to you angrily demanding that you talk him into getting treatment.

Husbands of addicts, on the other hand, are less likely to come for counseling. Usually you'll have to look for signs of a problem as you would with the addict. The wife attends church sporadically, perhaps. When you visit, she is often mysteriously "ill"—but you detect the odor of alcohol. So you talk to the husband about what you've observed and suggest that you and he get together.

Your counseling goals will be to help the counselee see the situation realistically, discover a course of action, learn basic coping skills, and enter further treatment. When you meet with the spouse, you may find that he or she only wants you to "fix" the other person. Your first obligation, however, is to help the person in front of you.

1. *Uncover the real problem.* The spouse may be reluctant to lay out the ugly facts right away. Conversation with a wife may go something like this:

"We're having problems in our marriage."

"What kind of problems?"

"He gets irritated with me. I just can't please him."

"Is it that you can't please him or that he can't be pleased?"

"I'm not sure. Maybe he just can't be pleased."

"Tell me more about your husband."

"He works hard to support us, and he's tired at night. He gets angry easily. But don't think he doesn't try to be a good husband and father."

"What does he do when he's tired?"

"Sometimes he does have a few beers."

"A few beers?"

"Well, sometimes more than a few."

"How does that make you feel?"

"I get really scared."

Draw a male spouse out the same way. Suppose Carl is meeting with you at your request. You begin talking about why his wife, Dina, has dropped out of church. Carl answers that she doesn't feel well much of the time. She's going through menopause and having a rough time.

When you ask if she's had medical help, he says yes, that a doctor gave her medication that includes tranquilizers. As you go into the subject more, Carl admits that she's getting prescriptions from several doctors for tranquilizers and taking far more than she should.

2. *Deal with roadblocks.* Here are some ways a spouse may deny the real source or severity of the situation—and some suggested responses.

- "It's my fault."

Say something like, "Some people seem to have a predisposition to addiction because it's handed down generationally. Sometimes, family traits do make it more likely that the individual will develop an addiction. Ultimately, though, he or she is the one who makes the choice to use the substance."

A phrase to use with any family member—adult or child—is this: "You didn't cause it; you can't cure it; but you can learn to cope with it."

- "It's not that bad." After the initial conversation, the spouse may back off and say, "I made too big a deal of it."

Say something like, "These are some of the things you said to me. [Then quote them to the person.] They seem pretty serious. What's happening now that you say it's not a big deal?" It will probably take a number of sessions to work though denial.

3. Evaluate the seriousness of the situation. Is the mate abusive? Is the spouse in danger? If that's the case, help the counselee make a plan. You may help her find a place she can stay temporarily, perhaps with a family in the church. However, if there is a chance, any chance whatsoever, that a physically abusive husband might come after her and/or the children, find a place of complete anonymity—probably out of town with no relative or friend connections. She shouldn't return home until she knows the situation is safe. In many areas there are shelters for women and children that can provide safe housing temporarily.

4. Find out what the family member is willing to do about the situation. If the addict is totally uncooperative, the spouse may choose to separate temporarily. But a wife who is dependent on her husband's financial support for herself and her children may feel she has no choice but to stay.

If the spouse remains too passive to take constructive action, ask, "How bad does it have to get before you'll do something to help yourself, your family, and your mate?"

One wife said, "If he sells drugs, that's where I draw the line." But when the husband did start selling drugs and the wife refused to admit it to herself, the counselor countered with, "Then selling drugs really isn't where you draw the line. Where is it, then?"

5. *Help the family members deal with their feelings.* Living with an addict causes the spouse to churn inside. He or she probably is having conflicting emotions. Ask, "How does your spouse's action make you feel?" Draw the counselee out and let him or her ventilate pent-up feelings. You may want to suggest that he or she keep a journal.

6. *Show ways to cope, not enable.* A spouse may try to show his or her love by protecting the chemically dependent mate from the consequences of his or her behavior. This is called "enabling," and the spouse is "the enabler."

Discuss the ways he or she has indeed protected the abuser from consequences—like filling prescriptions, cleaning up after her, buying beer, phoning his boss when he's too hung over to go to work. Show the spouse that the most loving thing to do is to make the addict experience the consequences of his or her actions because that will force the user to face the reality of the habit sooner.

Brainstorm ways to cope rather than to enable the mate to keep drinking or using drugs. You'll also want the family member to discover ways to stop building his or her life around the user's sick behavior. For example:

• Go to bed instead of staying up and pleading with the addict to stop drinking. Let him pass out on the sofa.

• Don't clean up after her if she soils herself as a result of being drunk or drugged.

• Refuse to lie for him. Tell the children what his real problem is.

• Focus on caring for yourself and your children instead of your spouse. Join an exercise class, take the kids camping, go out for dinner, etc.

• Remember that addicts make promises they don't keep. So demand the only action that counts: getting into treatment and working the prescribed program.

• Go into another room. Ignore him, and go on with things you need to do.

• Leave the house for a while until she calms down.

• Get a support group for your family. That may include a family at church who will take the children occasionally.

7. *Urge therapy.* Counseling will be available for all family members if the addict goes to a treatment center. Or the spouse can go for private counseling to someone trained and experienced in this area. A support group like Al-Anon or one sponsored by a church can also be helpful.

8. *Suggest that you visit the spouse together.* Do this only if the spouse is amenable to it, and only after the counselee's immediate needs have been met. When there, say something like, "I've been talking with your wife [husband], and she has a lot of concern about some things that are happening. We'd like to see if there's anything that either she or I or the church can do to help you through this."

Then you can turn to the spouse of the abuser and ask how he or she would describe the problem. The outcome of this kind of visit depends on the openness of the substance abuser.

Counseling a Parent

While parents probably come to see you because they need help for their child, the fact is that they need help themselves as well. Generally, it's in two areas.

1. *Denial.* "I can't believe this could happen in our family." "Why didn't I see what was going on?"

Direct the parent's thinking by showing why it can happen in any family and ask, "What in your life isn't allowing you to see this for what it is?" The answer might be something like: "I thought if I was a good enough Christian and prayed hard enough, things like this wouldn't happen." Or, "I never believed my daughter would use drugs."

Help the parent learn to see that it can happen to anyone and to look at the whole picture instead of seeing isolated incidents. A mother may say, "He said the marijuana belonged to someone else, and I believed him." Ask her what other changes she noticed in her son's life: falling grades, distancing himself, new friends, staying out more. Asking such questions can help break through denial.

2. Guilt. Show the parent how to differentiate between real guilt, which is the result of breaking one of God's laws, and false guilt—the product of distorted thinking. The parent may not get a clear picture of his or her involvement, however, until entering treatment with the child.

Begin to deal with real guilt by exploring the following areas:

• Tangible things the parent has done to support the child's habit, like deliberately ignoring signs of trouble.

• The family value system and moral standard—where has it been defective?

• Discipline methods—do they train the child or drive her farther into rebellion?

• What has been the effect of the decision-making process the family has modeled and taught?

• Has there been use of drugs and alcohol in the family that may have given permission?

Where real guilt exists, lead the parent to repent and forgive himself or herself. This includes changes in the offending behavior. When the guilt is false, help the parent to see why and to change his or her thought pattern.

Impress on the parent, though, that the child made an independent choice to use and keep using and needs to be responsible for the consequences of his or her actions.

Parents who throw themselves in front of a headstrong child to cushion him from his recklessness take the bruises, but the child learns nothing. Mom and dad can't be responsible for things over which they have no control.

Counseling a Child

A parent may bring a child for help, but more often that doesn't happen. One way to find these children in your congregation is to teach addiction prevention in Sunday school. Often a child comes up afterward and says, "That's happening at my house." Some suggested programs are outlined in Chapter 6.

You may also suspect a child is troubled from his or her behavior and move closer to the family to observe and help. Like the nonabusing spouse, children of addicts typically play certain roles in the family, too. Usually, such roles indicate that some kind of problem exists. Some you may observe are these:

• *The family hero*. This person is the overachiever who tries to do everything right. His or her goal is to prove that the family is normal: "Look at all my accomplishments."

• *The lost child*. This one rarely causes problems and never demands attention. He or she is too *nice* to be real.

• *The scapegoat*. This child is angry and defiant and does things wrong to relieve pressure on the family by placing attention on himself or herself.

• *The mascot*. This child distracts by acting silly or cute.

Help the child tell it like it is. If he or she comes to you with a parent, you might ask the parent to assure the child. "Say anything you'd like about the problem at home. This is your time."

The child will need to be given that permission to talk about the home problem because he or she has been living with three unspoken rules:

1. Don't talk. Of course the child talks but not about the substance abuser's problem and the effect on the family. "It's as though an elephant was sitting in the living room," write Jill Hastings and Marion Typpo. "No one acknowledges its presence, yet everyone makes allowances for it."

2. Don't trust. The addicted parent can't be trusted because he or she is generally undependable. The other parent may deny that a problem exists, even though the child senses that it does. As a result, the child learns not to trust any adult.

3. Don't feel. Carla's family pretended nothing was wrong, even though her father frequently passed out drunk on the sofa. Instead of admitting their own anxiety, the family members made fun of Carla because she was afraid. As a result, she learned to distrust her feelings and finally to pretend they didn't exist.

Break through denial. The child may not admit that addiction exists in the family, only that "I can't get along with my father." Probe beneath such a statement. "What kinds of problems do you and your dad have?"

"He yells at me a lot."

"When does he do that?"

"At dinner mostly."

"What's going on that he yells then?" Keep talking about what has been happening. Finally, the child may admit or come to see that it's because Dad is drunk.

Show that addiction is the parent's problem. "You didn't cause it; you can't cure it; but you can learn to cope with it."

Keep talking about how the family situation makes the child feel: guilty, insecure, afraid, etc. He or she needs to express feelings and be reminded that the situation isn't his or her fault. Dad's irrational behavior is a result of taking drugs and not anything the child has done. You'll probably have to restate that repeatedly.

One way to help a child is by using a "feelings poster."

It's a chart on which are drawn faces expressing various feelings like fear, confusion, embarrassment, etc. Children can point to ones they've felt and you can ask them to tell you more. You can make such a chart using simple, circular faces—or ask an artistic person in your church to make one for you.

Help the child discover options. Since he or she can't move out of the home, help the child think of ways to cope. Use the following as idea starters.

• Change the subject when there are arguments at dinner.

• If Dad hassles the child when the child sits at the dining room table doing homework, brainstorm another place to work.

• If there's no money for class trips and the like, think about ways the child can earn some. A teenager can get an after-school job. A younger child can get a paper route, do yard work, or work as a mother's helper—perhaps for people in the congregation. You can help a child find out whether the school has a fund for those who can't pay for special outings, etc. Your church might start a similar fund.

Report emergency situations. You can talk with the parents first, but you have absolutely no choice whether or not to report physical or sexual abuse or neglect to the children's protective agency in your area. It's the law, and it's the responsible thing to do. Failure to make such a report is to play the role of an enabler yourself. The abuser must face the consequences of his or her behavior.

Find a support group. Children can go with their parents to Al-Anon. Other groups are Alateen (for teenagers) and Alatot (for younger children). Or there may be a Christian support group in your area.

All family members will need ongoing care, and ways to do that will be discussed in Chapter 6.

Counseling the Adult Child

Left untreated, children of substance abusers carry their wounds into adulthood. They may become the next generation of codependents, passing on the legacy to their children. You can help prevent that by showing them the source of the problem and leading them into appropriate therapy.

Because of the plethora of publicity in recent years about adult children of addicts and the widespread anonymous support groups available, the adult children of substance abusers are the family members most likely to come for counseling. Specific problems they describe may include depression, feeling as though they don't fit anywhere, knowing they're unhappy but not knowing why, or experiencing anger they can't control.

Other symptoms you can expect to see are typical of people who come from homes in which life is abnormal. Some of the most common are having to guess what normalcy is, experiencing low self-esteem, judging themselves without mercy, having difficulty with intimate relationships, constantly seeking approval, feeling different, and demonstrating a need for immediate gratification.[2]

"Liontamers," the support group of the First Evangelical Free Church of Fullerton, California, describes the problem in the adult child's own words:

"We have acquired unhealthy ways of relating . . . we have stuffed our feelings from our traumatic childhood, and have lost the ability to feel or express our feelings . . . we became isolated and afraid of people and authority figures. Angry people and personal criticism frighten us . . . we either become alcoholics ourselves, or marry one, or both. Failing that, we find another compulsive personality such as a workaholic to fulfill our subconscious needs . . . we are terrified of abandonment."[3]

Ask about his or her past. After the person tells you why he or she has come for help, say, "This may not make much sense to you, but I'd like you to tell me what it was like when you were growing up." Probably the person will sugarcoat the account, so reflect back what he or she says until you get to the facts beneath the surface.

Show that the person's past affects the present. No matter who we are, that's true. A Christian counselee was forgiven and given a godly nature at his or her new birth. But he or she still is influenced by old thoughts and habit patterns and needs help discovering and dealing with them.

Laura may have told you that she's come for help because she yells at her kids all the time. During the session, you may discover that when she was growing up her mom yelled at her. Her dad was an alcoholic, and her mother was angry and took it out on the kids.

The reason Laura is verbally abusive is, at least in part, because she learned that kind of parenting from her mother. Mom yelled, so she yells. Besides, she probably is extremely angry at her dad for his alcoholic behavior and is hurting because he wasn't a real dad. Laura may be angry at her mom as well for taking her frustration out on Laura.

Get him or her started on the road to recovery. Liontamers provides some helpful guidelines.

1. "Even though their parents gave them physical existence, they can now look to God, their heavenly Father, as the Initiator of new life. They can look to Him to lead them to a new level of experience and give them direction toward a life of wholeness . . . they do not have to remain prisoners of their past.

2. "They can focus on themselves in the here and now, and detach from their obsession with the alcoholic. They can learn to love themselves and others, even though this may sometimes take the form of tough love.

3. "They can learn to allow themselves to feel their feelings and then to express them."

Provide the person with opportunities to accomplish what you determine together are his or her primary, immediate objectives. That may include a physical checkup, parenting classes, reading Bible-centered material on self-acceptance or anger or another subject and discussing it, or writing letters to his or her parents. Sometimes it is even valuable to write letters that are left unsent, just to let facts and feelings out.

Those who need to explore more deeply the specific ways in which their background has affected them may require private, professional counseling at this point. Dealing with denial, codependency, and their role as enablers will probably take time.

It's likely to be helpful for them to be part of a support group—one sponsored by a church perhaps—or an Adult Children of Alcoholics chapter. Keep in mind that individuals and groups vary, so you should do some investigation before recommending any. These groups are not therapy in the pure sense because most do not have a professional facilitating the meeting. They are, however, what their name implies: support by people who share like experiences.

Spiritual Teaching to Aid Recovery

Subjects with which most family members will need special help include these:

1. Faith. Life has been unpredictable and trust has been eroded. Help them see that in contrast, God is loving, benevolent, and completely trustworthy.

2. Relationships. Family members haven't experienced normal relationships and can benefit from understanding biblical patterns and how to live them out in daily life. Especially important is an accurate interpretation of submission, which may have been tainted with abuse.

3. Communication with God. They'll need to learn how

to tell God everything and cast all their cares on Him. In this way, they'll begin to establish the intimacy with their heavenly Father that they desperately need.

In addition, urge them to take advantage of opportunities to internalize the basic Bible doctrines everyone needs to know. This is especially important; even if family members have been involved in church programs, they've probably heard doctrine through the internal filter that people in their situation possess.

CHAPTER SIX

THE CHURCH AND SUBSTANCE ABUSE

ADDICTS AND THEIR FAMILIES NEED THE HELP OF THE whole church to recover. Paul lays down the principles for members' participation when he points out, "There should be no division in the body, but . . . its parts should have equal concern for each other" (I Cor. 12:25).

That includes leadership from the Christian education department, Bible study groups, visitation teams, youth workers, and hospitality committees as well as the pastor. But it's not enough for leaders alone to be prepared; the average congregational member must be prepared also.

This chapter is divided into three sections: prevention, intervention, and postvention (or aftercare). Suggestions are made that enable the church to contribute in these areas.

Prevention

Here the church can be most effective by doing two things: (1) initiating substance abuse prevention programs for all ages and (2) building Christian personhood and community.

Plan specific ways to teach those in your church about alcohol and drugs and their effects on the user and those close to the user. The most efficient way to go about this is through programs geared to each age level.

Even younger children can be taught to respect and care for their bodies and not to do anything to harm them. As soon as they're exposed to the fact of drugs in their world, they can be given information about these substances and how to avoid use.

PRIMARIES AND JUNIORS

Use the following material for a special presentation during Sunday school, a club program, or another time when children meet separately from adults.

Preparation: Glean information about drugs and their effects from this book and material listed in the bibliography. Also collect magazine pictures, paper, scissors, and glue for collages.

Presentation: Discuss drugs the children already know about that are an everyday part of life—such as aspirin for headaches, cold tablets, etc. Talk about the kinds of drugs that are good for us, like the doctor's medicine and over-the-counter preparations taken at specific times for specific ailments. Ask the children if any of them have had to take medicines that the doctor has prescribed for them.

Then talk about the kinds of drugs that are bad for us like cigarettes, marijuana, cocaine, etc. Talk about some of the reasons they're bad for us.

Next, talk about how the media presents the use of drugs to us. Have the children make collages from magazine pictures advertising various drugs. Include all kinds, good and bad: caffeine, cold remedies, pain medications, alcohol, and nicotine. Discuss implications of the collages. Do the ads help us decide what's good and bad? Do they make the bad drugs look fun?

Then explain how some harmful drugs make the user feel good for a while; that's the first result. But the second result is to do increasingly serious harm. Talk about some of the bad things drugs can do to us. To demonstrate this, try the following exercise.

Game: Form a loose circle with one person in the middle who represents a person using drugs. Have him or her try to escape. Guide the children to let that person succeed. Then explain that this is how it is with some drugs at first. Then have the "user" re-enter the circle. This time instruct the children to tighten the circle, possibly locking arms. Explain that some drugs, like crack, trap the user right away while others drugs do so after continued use. Explain what it means to be addicted.

Exercise: Help the children learn how to respond if tempted to use these kinds of drugs. Emphasize quick and complete refusals. (Refusals are more complete if the person leaves the situation immediately.) Have the children role-play their answers to situations like these:

• Your best friend offers you a bottle of beer.

• Your uncle offers you a marijuana cigarette.

• Your friend's mom leaves the liquor cabinet open; your friend helps herself, then calls you a chicken if you don't have some, too.

Advise the children that if they are offered drugs or alcohol, they should tell a trusted adult. Assure them that this is not being a tattletale. Drugs and alcohol can hurt them, their friends, or family members, so they'll be doing what's best for everyone.

Conclusion: Remind the children that their bodies are a gift from God, a miracle that He wants them to protect. He has made us for a purpose and wants us to take care of our bodies so that we can fulfill that mission (Eph. 2:10). Then pray with the children for strength, and remind them that they can always count on God's help.

Option: Choose a film from the bibliography in the back of this book and follow with a discussion that includes the biblical perspective.

YOUTH

Use the following material for a special presentation during Sunday school, a youth group meeting, or a retreat.

Preparation: Videotape or just watch some anti-drug television commercials so you can lead a discussion as to whether or not they're effective and why. Collect newspaper clippings of drug and/or alcohol-related crimes or accidents in your area. Then cover the following points in the presentation:

1. *Know what's true and what's not.* Form teams to compete against one another or have each student take a true-or-false test. Draw up a list of statements from information in this book, such as "Teenagers become addicted to alcohol faster than adults" (true; metabolized faster). "Marijuana is not addictive" (false; psychologically addictive).

Discuss how important it is to know the truth about drugs and alcohol. Mention that in a recent Gallup poll, four million youth between thirteen and seventeen said they'd been offered illegal drugs in the past thirty days. Refer to newspaper clippings and discuss the prevalence of drug and alcohol use in your area.

Find out what your young people know about addiction and the effects of particular drugs and alcohol. Provide correct information where needed.

Point out that drugs and alcohol may be pleasurable at first but later can cause physical, mental, emotional, and spiritual deterioration. Also say that the user may become less attractive; weight change and poor complexion, for example, can result. Ask the kids what they think about such denial statements as, "It won't happen to me." Discuss the validity of their answers.

2. *Know where you stand.* If you taped anti-drug television commercials, view them and discuss with the group why the ads are or are not effective. Ask what things the group would say to convince other teens not to use drugs. Have the group brainstorm ideas for a high-impact anti-drug TV commercial.

3. *What biblical principles motivate you to be drug-free?* You and the group might bring up the fact that our bodies are the temple of the Holy Spirit, that abusing drugs or alcohol isn't acting lovingly toward ourselves, that it's

against the law, that we're being disobedient to our parents, etc. Refer to Chapter 4 for additional material.

4. *Make a personal commitment now.* It's too dangerous to wait until temptation hits and then hope you can "just say no." Each person needs to make a commitment to stay drug-free now. Point out that only individuals can make the choice, and that in so doing they will be making a decision that affects their whole future. Encourage such a prayer of commitment, publicly in the group if possible.

Optional: To reinforce the personal commitments the teens make, have them design T-shirts, buttons, or banners with an "I choose to be drug-free" slogan. Or encourage them to plan anti-drug skits or puppet shows to put on for other age groups.

5. *Know what to say.* Use the stories of LuAnn, Gordon, and Dan (Chapters 1 and 2) and have the group brainstorm ways to deal with the temptation to try drugs. Point out the necessity of standing by one's commitment, of praying for strength, and for giving a quick and complete refusal when offered drugs.

Emphasize the importance of leaving the scene immediately—no matter where the scene is. There is often a subtle but dangerous compromise involved in remaining with people who are using drugs, even if attempting to say no personally. In some cases one may risk legal consequences if the group is arrested. But even when that does not happen, staying with those who are using greatly softens one's refusal. It's as though one were saying, "It's okay with me if *you* do it; it's just not *my* thing." The next step is to be challenged with, "If it's okay, why not try it? Maybe you'll like it." That dialog may not occur, but the implications of it are present.

6. *Know where to get help.* Remind the young people that no one's perfect. Anyone may give in to temptation. Share something like this: "If you are using drugs or alcohol now,

here are some steps to take:

• Face facts. You have a problem.

• Get help. Come to me or another mature, nonaddicted adult.

• Ask God for forgiveness and forgive yourself (I John 1:9).

• Renew your commitment, and take whatever action is necessary to avoid temptation, such as cutting off drug-using friends and making drug-free ones.

• Stay close to God. Practice making prayer an ongoing conversation with Him. Learn His promises to help you (I Cor. 10:13; Heb. 2:18)."

ADULTS

Option 1: Have a panel discussion. Include some or all of the following:

• A physician or pharmacologist to give information about various drugs, their effects, and the dangers involved.

• A psychologist or other professional counselor experienced in treating addiction to discuss the psychological aspects and the way to recovery.

• A pastor to present the biblical view.

• Someone formerly addicted to drugs or alcohol.

• The spouse or child of an addict, now in recovery.

• A law enforcement officer familiar with drug and alcohol abuse problems.

Option 2: Use material in this book and others listed in the bibliography to create a teaching session based on the following:

1. Chemically-inclined society. We live in a drug culture. We use, among other substances, caffeine and over-the-counter preparations to self-medicate. Our lifestyle suggests it's okay to use a drug to get started in the morning or to wind down at night. What message do we send one another and our children by this practice?

2. *Information about drugs and alcohol, and their effects.*
Explain physiological and psychological addiction.

3. *Discuss the formation of personal family value systems
as they relate to drug use.* That includes viewing use of
legitimate medications as a help provided by God, our attitude of respect for our bodies, and our attitude and personal
use of alcohol and illegal drugs. Each person should assess
his or her own behavior.

4. *Point out who is most in danger of addiction.* Emphasize that those who'll become addicted can't be predicted.
Some, though, as pointed out in this book, fall into a high-
risk group. (See Chapter 8 and the question about those most
likely to become substance abusers.)

5. *Learn to live the way God intended, not dependent on
substances to get through life.* Instead, look for natural
means of relieving stress such as relaxation, exercise, and
hobbies. Also plan healthy ways to experience excitement,
like accomplishing a task that seemed impossible (going
back to school, for example) or helping someone else (Matt.
6:25-34; Matt. 11:28; John 15:5; John 10:10).

6. *Take precautions to keep your children drug-free.*
• Talk with them about drug use.
• Realize that no child is immune.
• Provide positive peer groups and adult role models.
• Introduce them to healthy activities that match their in-
terests and abilities.
• Learn to listen to them.
• Know behavior patterns that may be a sign that some-
thing's wrong.
• If you suspect your child is using, talk with him or her
about what you see and immediately take whatever steps
are necessary.
• Follow the procedure outlined in Chapter 3.

FOR ALL AGES

Emphasize the following among all ages:

1. Personal worth (Ps. 8; Ps. 139; Eph. 1:3-14; I John 3:1).

2. God as living companion and present help (Matt. 6:25-34; 28:20b; John 14:16-18).

3. A sense of community (Acts 2:42-47; Romans 12:4, 5; I Cor. 12:12-26). Experiment with small groups, prayer partners, and discipling programs to provide closeness.

4. Intergenerational fellowship—times when children, youth and adults work/play/study together. Try work days, talent nights, community projects.

In addition, provide courses that help build strong families and smooth the way through traumatic life transitions. Have your Christian education committee review curriculum that addresses human transitions such as early parenting, parenting adolescents, dealing with mid-life, and retirement issues. One helpful series for adults is the Family Ministry Electives from the David C. Cook Publishing Co.:

On My Own: A Course for Young Singles
Newly Married: A Course to Build Foundations
Now There Are Three: A Course for New Parents
Big People, Little People: A Course for Parents
Just Me and the Kids: A Course for Single Parents
You and Your Teen: A Course for Mid-Life Christians
Empty Nest: Life After the Kids Leave Home
The Freedom Years: A Celebration of Retirement.

It's during life's crises that individuals tend to turn toward drugs and alcohol as stress relievers. Also emphasize personal growth, understanding among family members, and problem-solving techniques. Develop a long-range program to cover key issues.

Intervention

Christians will have an opportunity to sense others' addiction-related problems when they're living in community. If Christians are humble, not thinking more highly of themselves than they ought, they'll be approachable.

1. Make sure the people in your church know they can discuss their own problems with church leaders and that they can ask leaders to intervene when others are in crisis.

2. Emphasize the need for loving confrontation. Shielding a person who's in trouble instead of going for help isn't the loving thing to do.

3. Families in treatment may need child care, food, clothing, or shelter if they've had to leave an abusive situation. John's admonition is apt: "Dear children, let us not love with words or tongue but with actions and in truth" (I John 3:18).

Your church can also establish a fund to help subsidize counseling or provide for other related needs. Larger churches that have a staff counselor can use such a fund to allow for a reduced fee when necessary.

4. Both the addict and the family in treatment will need emotional and spiritual support. Cards, phone calls, visits, and invitations to get together are vital. These hurting people will be dealing with patterns deeply rooted in their psyches that have had a painful effect. Church members need to understand and not pressure sufferers to be what they can't be at this stage. Acceptance will promote healing.

Now, and throughout the process, the family will need the prayers of the church. Not that their problems should be announced from the pulpit on Sunday morning; use discretion and have the permission of the individuals involved. When they understand that prayers of believers are powerful and effective (Jas. 5:16) and that they are continually being brought before God, they will be strengthened.

Postvention or Aftercare

For the abuser and family, putting one foot in front of the other every day can be tough enough without finding support trickling away because Christians think the problem "should be solved by now." Responsibility can be delegated to specific individuals to be sure these families don't slip between the cracks.

The abusers have been directed to drop old, drug-using friends and make new ones. Help them do that by drawing them into men's or women's groups, Bible studies, and support groups.

Find out what their talents are and offer opportunities to serve in the church. A person who is mechanically-minded can work on the church van; a good cook can help plan a church dinner. Being needed does much to enhance self-esteem.

Teens need to contribute, too. Provide work that counts—like acting in a church play, singing in a cantata, or working with a group doing yard or home repair work for shut-ins.

Children from addicted families will benefit from time spent in healthy homes. Being with people who can express their emotions constructively can help build up these children.

Be especially sensitive at holiday times. For a variety of reasons, holidays are often very difficult for recovering abusers and family members of addicts or former addicts. Make sure some Christians stay close at that time, perhaps inviting recovering addicts or family members to go on a Fourth of July picnic or to attend a Christmas party.

Starting a Support Group

Your church may want to sponsor a Bible-based support group that focuses on the Lord Jesus Christ as the One on whom the individual can depend for help in recovery. Although you may also sponsor groups for family members of addicts, the following guidelines are for beginning a recovery group for the substance abuser.

Choosing a leader. If the person is a recovered addict, he or she should have been sober at least two years, should have been working a recovery program, and should be making personality changes with significant success. He or she should have been part of an "anonymous" group and have a broad knowledge of addiction and its treatment. Equally important is the leader's spiritual maturity and ability to disciple others.

The leader also may be an empathetic nonaddict who is spiritually mature and has completed training as an alcohol and drug counselor in a community college or a private institution. Whoever the leader, he or she will need an assistant who's able to take over when needed.

Getting started. Those organizing the group should consult with a professional counselor experienced in treating addiction. He or she can help set up a format and guidelines. The leader should consult the counselor any time he or she needs more information.

Getting members. The nucleus will probably come from your church. Ask other churches to inform their congregations about the group. Also contact Christian counselors and physicians in your area.

Format. Most groups are set up around Alcoholics Anonymous' Twelve Step program, adding related Scripture. See the Appendix and Bibliography for information to help you do that.

You may want to divide your meeting time into two one-hour sessions. The first would be teaching and education. A speaker would address various addiction-related subjects. Speakers or resources might include counselors, pastors, physicians, ex-addicts long recovered who have also experienced positive personality changes, films, panels, or round-table discussions.

The second part of the meeting would be for small-group sharing. Each person would use only his or her first name. Open with prayer, greet and acknowledge new people and returnees, share the purpose of the group and its rules and goals, having someone read these. Emphasize confidentiality.

Allow people to talk about what is on their minds. That includes their struggles and the phase of recovery through which they are working. Especially encourage members to tell what they are doing to get well. If things start slowly, the leader can talk about some new thing he or she is learning. Limit each person's time to five minutes or so.

While members are not present to "fix" one another, they can respond by telling how they relate to what has been said and what they have learned on their own journey. Discourage moralizing, preaching, and judgmental comments. Help people remember to speak in the first person instead of the third.

The leader acts as facilitator and guide. He or she keeps the meeting moving, handles difficult situations (someone riding a doctrinal hobby horse, for instance), keeps Jesus Christ as the "Higher Power" central. The leader assures that it's permissible to cry or express anger, but remains in charge of volatile situations.

When necessary, arrange to speak privately with a group member who seems to need special help. Don't expect to have all the answers. In her *Guidelines for a Successful Small Group*, Sue Jenkis says, "It is not necessary or possible to always come to a final conclusion—that is not the point. Sharing, learning, growing and loving together from the Word of God is the purpose."

CHAPTER SEVEN

ADDICTION AND THE LAW

W HEN FAMILY MEMBERS RECEIVE THE DREADED PHONE call that someone they love has been arrested for an alcohol- or drug-related crime, naturally they are devastated. Most have never had dealings with the criminal justice system and have no idea what to expect.

This chapter provides an overview of what they may face. You can use this information to acquaint the family with the process. The chapter also describes specific ways in which you can help. However, the information should not be used in place of legal counsel and does not apply where local laws and procedures vary.

From Church Pew to Prison

Gordon, who grew up in church (his story was told in Chapter 1), has a long history of alcohol-related arrests. His case illustrates the legal problems to which addiction may lead. "When I was eighteen, I shot a guy," Gordon says. "It was an accident, and I was acquitted, but it wouldn't have happened if I hadn't been drinking."

On other occasions, he did serve time in jail on disorderly conduct charges and lost his license for a year for driving under the influence—a charge that was compounded by the fact that he had acquired a stack of speeding tickets.

"But when I was twenty-nine years old, I got in serious trouble," he says. "I'd consumed close to a fifth of tequila and had eaten eight or nine peyote buttons. In addition, I'd been taking speed." In his drunken and drugged state he broke into a woman's house.

The woman happened to be talking to her boyfriend on the phone at the time, and he called the police. "By the time they arrived, I'd passed out cold," Gordon says. "I came to in jail and was charged with breaking and entering and attempted rape. The police dropped the rape charge, but I was sentenced to four years for breaking and entering.

"I served a little over two years of the sentence, and my folks stood by me through it all. . . . Other guys said they were [in prison] because someone turned them in or the judge had it in for them. One day it hit me: I'm here because I committed a crime." Fortunately for Gordon, prison life jolted him into thinking straighter than he had in years.

When someone has been arrested, one of the first things the family must determine is the nature of the charge. This is the first step in understanding the legal process that will follow.

Misdemeanors

Misdemeanors are crimes that involve lesser offenses, for which the maximum penalty is one year or less. These include such things as petty theft, intentionally damaging someone's property, knowingly writing a bad check, and assault.

An adult who is arrested for a misdemeanor often receives a citation requiring him or her to appear in court on the specified date. If the case is to be defended, legal fees for a misdemeanor can run from hundreds to thousands of dollars. If the case involves a jury trial, the total cost in attorney fees could total from two to three thousand dollars.

Public drunkenness, which used to be one of the most common crimes, is no longer against the law in some areas. Those who are publicly intoxicated may be picked up if they endanger themselves or others and may be remanded for detoxification. Possession of a controlled substance, as well as buying or selling it, is illegal, of course. Driving while under the influence is also a crime, and one that is being treated with increasing seriousness.

"There has been a dramatic shift in how we deal with driving under the influence," says attorney James Brown. A former district attorney, he points out that in the past it seemed almost impossible to prosecute such cases successfully. Jurors would be asked, "Haven't you driven with one drink more than you should have?" But today, Brown says, "Successful prosecution is the rule rather than the exception."

Depending on the situation, offenders could lose their licenses temporarily, have their driving restricted, or lose their licenses permanently. Bodily injury to others as a result of driving under the influence is a more serious complication.

Diversion programs, in which the individual is committed to enter a treatment program for substance abuse, are often made available for first offenders. Programs may be offered through a county mental health agency, a private institution, a for-profit institution, or a private nonprofit institution.

One example: On a weekend, after drinking heavily for two days, Gordon was arrested for disorderly conduct. He became violent during the arrest and attacked a police officer. After he was placed in a patrol car, he kicked out a window and smashed the police radio. He was booked on additional charges: resisting arrest, attacking a police officer, and destroying public property.

On Monday he appeared before a judge and pleaded not guilty. The same day, he used his phone call to engage an attorney two friends had used and found satisfactory. After four days in jail, very high bail was set, but his attorney managed to get Gordon released on his own recognizance.

About a month later, his case was heard. The judge fined him $800 plus $285 to pay for the damages to the police car. The attorney fee was $800, and he lost six days of work. The incident cost him well over $2,000.

Felonies

A felony is a crime that is punishable in a penitentiary for more than one year. Crimes considered to be felonies include burglaries, sexual assaults, and crimes which are against persons and which involve weapons. Since vehicles can function as weapons, injury to another—especially when driving under the influence of drugs or alcohol—can be treated as a felony assault in death cases such as manslaughter, or sometimes negligent homicide.

"Felony crimes take in a fair amount of territory," comments attorney Brown. "The likelihood that the individual will be taken into custody is fairly high." Whether or not that happens may depend on the jail space in your area.

Drug- and alcohol-related laws vary from state to state. While there are similarities, no two states are identical in all respects. Check laws on specific crimes in your area.

Legal fees for felonies can be very high. Families often must resort to taking out a second mortgage on their homes and/or withdrawing their savings or retirement funds.

When the Accused Can't Afford an Attorney

In all cases except minor traffic violations, the court will appoint an attorney if the accused can't afford one. For that to happen, the person must fill out an affidavit stating his or her resources. If he or she qualifies, a lawyer is appointed to defend the person throughout the trial process.

Bail

In some states, the old bail bondsman system has been replaced. Now the one posting bail is required to put up ten percent of the amount. So for bail of $5,000, the individual would need to post $500, usually in cash. If the accused skips town, whoever posts bail is liable for the whole sum. It's important to be familiar with the bail system in effect in your area.

The decision as to whether or not to release an individual on bail is made, for one thing, by determining his or her risk of flight. If the person has family in the community, owns property there, or has other ties to the community, he or she is more likely to be released than would be someone who is just passing through.

What Kind of Sentence?

For a felony, probation is possible if a modest first offense is involved. "Jail time as a condition of probation is fairly likely," Brown comments. "The judge may believe that the individual—particularly a young person—needs to know what it feels like to be confined. Restitution is also more and more an objective as well."

Youth and the Law

An offender under eighteen years of age may be treated as a juvenile or remanded to adult court, depending on the seriousness of the offense. If chemical dependency is part of the situation, the juvenile court may retain jurisdiction and require counseling, perhaps placing the youth in foster care or even ordering time in detention as part of the remedial program.

While the parent can request help from the court for the chemically dependent child, what's available may be limited because of the system's overcrowdedness. The parent may be better off researching private help available, and the helper can assist.

Four Ways You Can Help

1. When an addict is arrested—unless he or she is a chronic offender and help is inadvisable—urge the family

to obtain the services of an attorney who handles such cases if the family can afford one and the offense calls for it.

The family may need you to recommend legal counsel, so try to find out about attorneys in your area who could defend such cases. "In some respects, I liken [selecting a good attorney] to picking out a counselor," Brown says. "Ask around. Talk to friends. Interview prospective lawyers. Ask yourself: Is this someone with whom we can communicate? Someone who has a good reputation and experience in this particular kind of legal practice?"

Be aggressive in the selection process, Brown urges. It's more important to choose someone whom others can vouch for as competent than it is to choose someone who has a "big name."

Advise family members to select an attorney who has a fee schedule that is within their range. They should understand what it is that they're buying. They can ask, "How do you charge? Are phone calls, photocopies, secretarial expenses, mileage, and paralegal fees billed separately?"

Ask questions to help the family decide how much legal aid they can give. While a family member might like to say, "Cost is no object when it comes to getting my loved one out," it is still necessary to be practical. Expending all available resources may jeopardize the family's future in other ways.

There may be a time when the family has to refuse to obtain legal counsel for an addict who has been arrested. One mother said, "I got to the place where I felt that I was only contributing to my son's problem by getting him out of trouble. He's sober now, but during those earlier years, I had to learn to practice tough love because the addiction cycle kept repeating itself. It was heartbreaking." Such family members may need your insight and reinforcement.

If the family can't afford an attorney and needs one, be sure to ask the court to appoint one.

2. Suggest that the offender seek counseling and/or treatment immediately. Brown says, "When a friend called recently because a family member had an alcohol-related legal problem, I told them, 'Get on this right away.' . . . I did recommend that he not wait until a judge ordered rehabilitation for the offender." This response has two benefits. It may show the judge that the offender is serious about changing, which may work in the defendant's favor, and it is wise to seize the opportunity to begin recovery for the addict's sake. It is at this moment that the addict has been most shockingly shown that he or she has a problem. Denial is no longer as simple as it once was or will be several weeks later when the sting of the arrest has worn off.

3. A legal crisis is also the time for the rest of the family to deal with other issues related to substance abuse. A juvenile's problems may be compounded by the fact that Dad's work takes him out of town all the time, and, as a result, Mom and Dad may not be getting along. If ever there's a time to get on these things, it's now. "It's either pay me now or pay me later," Brown adds. Treatment can include counseling, probably in an alcohol and drug center, and participation in a support group.

4. Provide ongoing support for offender and family. Visits to the offender in jail or prison by those who are mature can be a good idea. See if the offender would like good reading material. If the institution allows one-on-one Bible study, find out if the person is open to that. Help the prisoner make constructive choices. Remain supportive as long as it helps, rather than hinders, the person's progress. Make sure the offender has caring Christians to contact when he or she is released from jail or prison.

Find out what the family's greatest needs are and act out your concern in practical ways. For example, family members may want you to go with them to court. They may be without funds to live on. Pray regularly for them—and with them if they're amenable. Other suggestions that apply are given in Chapter 6.

Regardless of how repentant the offender may be, everyone involved must face the fact that to break the law has legal consequences. Dealing with those consequences is one of the hardest things family members will have to do. But you and others in the church can help them maintain their equilibrium through the difficult process.

Express a noncondemnatory tone if the worst scenario is played out and the loved one is sent to jail or the penitentiary. Help the family members see the positive side of the situation, despite all the negatives. Time behind bars could be the crisis that leads to the ultimate turn-around in the life of the addict.

CHAPTER EIGHT

QUESTIONS AND ANSWERS

F ROM TIME TO TIME BOTH YOU AND THE PEOPLE YOU counsel will have questions. This chapter provides general answers to many of the questions most commonly asked. These answers can also be used as part of the substance abuse educational program in your church.

Questions about Addiction

Is alcoholism a disease?

It's a disease in the sense that it attacks a person and is degenerative. However, it's not a disease in the sense that it takes over a person without that person making choices that allow it to happen. The addict chooses to use and keep using even though, in our society, we know the dangers of drugs and alcohol. If the individual doesn't seek recovery, it's because he or she has chosen not to do so.

The "disease" concept can be used to allow a person to escape moral responsibility. Some who are adamant about that concept are reacting to those who foster the idea that the addict is a bad person instead of a person who does bad things.

Are addicts just undisciplined?

That's too simplistic. Some, for example, are professionals who are extremely disciplined and successful in other areas of their lives—until they deteriorate because of their habit.

Still, they develop an uncontrollable addiction.

Is addiction the result of demon possession?

Generally not. Obviously, Satan's going to try to encourage that kind of behavior, so he's likely to tempt the person to start and keep using. But he has no power over us that we don't give him. To blame it all on Satan is to remove personal responsibility.

Can't God just remove the craving?

Of course. Sometimes He heals a person instantly. Other times He gives partial healing. For example, an individual may be addicted to drugs and alcohol or drugs and gambling. The craving for drugs may be removed, but the addiction to alcohol or gambling as well as the addictive personality may remain.

Sometimes God apparently wants the person to take the traditional route to recovery. The Holy Spirit decides, based on the person's total needs. Instantaneous healing, for some individuals, seems not to be the best answer—because for them what comes cheaply goes cheaply. Such a person may need to take the slower, more arduous course.

How can a Christian become an addict?

Christians are subject to the same internal and external pressures as non-Christians. Some may have a genetic predisposition; all Christians have the normal dependent response to addictive drugs. Like non-Christians, if they use a drug that makes them feel good temporarily, they want to repeat the experience, and it can become a habit.

Scripture verifies Christians' vulnerability when it points out that even people who have a relationship with Jesus Christ struggle with the imperfections of the flesh. Paul describes this fact in Romans 7:22, 23. "For in my inner being I delight in God's law; but I see another law at work in the members of my body, waging war against the law of my mind and making me a prisoner of the law of sin at work within my members."

James 1:5 makes it clear that the way to handle life is to ask God for wisdom. Problems come when we insist on handling trouble without God.

How can I tell if a person is addicted to drugs or alcohol?

Here are some questions to ask in making that assessment:

1. Can the person stop using the substance of choice for a prolonged period of time? If he or she does quit, are there any withdrawal symptoms?

2. Has use of the substance interfered with business, social, or family relationships?

3. Is the person very defensive about the use of the substance—including vigorous denial of any problem?

4. Has he or she shown signs of physical or mental deterioration since beginning to use the substance (e.g., memory loss, blackouts, stomach problems)?

5. Does the person seem to be withdrawing from those who don't use the same substances in the same way?

6. Does the person use the substance often—perhaps more than three times a week?

7. Does he or she consistently use enough of the substance to induce intoxication or a high each time in spite of promises to refrain?

In addition, you may obtain pamphlets with a more detailed list of symptoms from organizations that deal with addiction. See the Bibliography.

Why is it wrong to smoke marijuana very occasionally?

The person who does so is opening himself or herself to potential psychological addiction, and no one can predict to whom that will happen. A young person who has problems and uses it to escape those problems may well become hooked. One who has low self-esteem and trouble making friends may escalate usage to keep up with drug-using peer group members. And, while not everyone who uses marijuana goes on to harder drugs, most who do use hard drugs began with marijuana.

Besides the psychologically addictive nature of the drug, using it is illegal. Then there's the fact that it puts the user in contact with people who may only be interested in selling him or her more drugs.

Since the effect of marijuana for many is to tranquilize, it can prevent emotional maturation because the person isn't becoming honed by life experiences. In addition, studies over nearly twenty years have shown that marijuana causes physiological damage as well—the potential for short-term memory loss, severe anxiety attacks, lowered sperm count, and an even higher risk of cancer than with tobacco smoke. In comparison to the "grass" of twenty years ago, today's hybrid marijuana can be like whiskey compared to beer; most of it is extremely strong.

Is the person who goes on binges an addict?

One form of alcoholism is episodic drinking. Jim may be cold sober except for once a month or so, when he drinks until he blacks out. What's important isn't how frequently he abuses alcohol—once a day or once a month—but the repetitious nature of the act.

Should I contact a counselee's doctor if I suspect she's addicted to prescription drugs?

Yes. For example, if a woman comes for help and you suspect she's addicted to sleeping pills, call her physician and tell what you've observed. If you suspect she's getting medication from more than one doctor, say so. In some cities, physicians can check drug stores the counselee normally uses for multiple prescriptions.

Or, perhaps a man comes to see you because he's experiencing anxiety and asks you to talk with his doctor so he'll prescribe tranquilizers. (The physician has previously refused.) Call, but ask the physician to evaluate the patient for potential addiction or suggest he remain cautious in prescribing.

What groups of people are most likely to become substance abusers?

1. Some may have a genetic predisposition, although that hasn't been proven conclusively yet. Researchers at the University of California at Los Angeles reportedly have found that a certain gene appears commonly in alcoholics. They have yet to establish that the gene causes alcoholism, however. Those whose caregivers modeled addictive behavior certainly are more likely to adopt it themselves.

2. People with emotional disorders such as depression or anxiety may self-medicate with alcohol or drugs.

3. Those with severe mental disorders such as schizophrenia may do the same thing.

4. Those who have a poor sense of identity may use addictive substances to bolster themselves.

5. Those who are passive-dependent and don't handle life very easily may come to depend on alcohol or drugs.

6. Those who are compulsive in other areas of their lives may find themselves returning to addictive substances again and again.

Once an addict always an addict?

There should be a time—after five years or so—when the individual is considered more well than not. There's a danger that the person might make "addict" his or her personal identity. Instead, it's important to grow beyond that.

Of course, the person *does* have a history of addiction and a propensity toward it (although everyone has the potential, to some degree). So whatever substance the person has abused must be considered off limits. No matter how confident the person may feel because he or she has been clean and sober a long time, using the substance again is taking a big chance. That's not a reflection on his or her character, simply a safeguard. Of course, all illegal drugs are off limits anyway.

Questions about Treatment

What does "working the program" mean?

The "program" is the Twelve Steps initially designed by Alcoholics Anonymous, on which most anonymous, self-help groups are based. To "work the program," a person thinks deeply about each step and learns how to apply it in specific ways. Usually the person is working to apply a particular step in an effective and complete manner.

Doing so becomes part of the way he or she lives and, as a result, the individual experiences growth and recovery. The goal is for these steps to become habit. The person receives help from his or her sponsor (a person in the group who is farther along in the recovery process) as well as from others in the group.

How can I help substance abusers who are elderly?

Often the problem is a response to loneliness and loss—physical, intellectual, and social. Such loss can be overwhelming. The counseling steps are the same, but be sure to find out whether the person has nutritional problems.

The church can be of particular help by compensating for the isolation the person feels as well as by providing for other specific needs. In this way, you'll be removing some of the reasons for abusing substances in the first place.

Do addicts have to go to support groups all their lives?

They certainly need a support group, but it's a good idea for them to build an adequate one among Christian friends so they don't have to go to a special place for support indefinitely. All Christians can benefit from this kind of support. On the other hand, attendance at an anonymous group can be very helpful even after being clean and sober for years because it provides an opportunity to help others. Sharing what a person has learned with those new in recovery can be valuable for both parties.

I Corinthians 10:13 says that when we're tempted God will provide a way out so we can stand up under the temptation. What's the way out for an addict?

The first way out that God provides is to give the individual the opportunity to turn to Him, admit the addiction, and ask for help. After the person walks through that door, other doors open up. They include:

• The knowledge that the all-powerful God is ready and willing to help.

• God's continual renewal that leads to freedom from old, debilitating concepts.

• The ability to cultivate a group of supportive, encouraging fellow believers.

• Access through prayer to a Savior who was tempted in the same way we are tempted.

When should church discipline be used?

Formal church discipline should be used only after everything else has failed—and then only after much prayer. Loving confrontation, intervention, and all the other procedures recommended in this book should be tried first. If the problem persists and is public and you do decide on church discipline, remember that *its purpose is to restore the person to fellowship with God.*

Use Matthew 18:15-17 as the format. Talk with the person privately. If that fails to produce positive results, take one or two people along and talk again. Only after exhausting each step outlined should you consider disfellowship.

The worst approach would be to show up on the person's doorstep cold and say, "You're out!" That would be destructive, not restorative.

How do I deal with an addict who promises to change but never does so for more than a few weeks?

Recognize that the person is either making promises with no intention of keeping them and still hasn't taken responsibility for his or her behavior. Or the person is equating intentions with the actions—as though the promise was as good as the behavior change. He or she is still locked in distorted thinking and denial.

Confront the person with the fact that promises haven't led to action. Be specific in the action you expect; for example, entering a treatment program and following up with the therapy and support group attendance that the professionals involved recommend.

Questions about Youth and Substance Abuse

Does a teen have the right to refuse treatment?

In this country, we have a legal concept called "the age of consent." A child below whatever age that is in your state is considered not to have the maturity to make adult decisions. The parent becomes legally responsible for the child's treatment up to that age.

Is it a good idea to lock out a teen who repeatedly comes home drunk and refuses treatment?

That has to be applied carefully, case by case, because it can do harm as well as good. If a parent hasn't taken responsibility for supervision for a long time, giving the child an insecure base, hardening one's spine can be helpful. On the other hand, radical techniques often appeal to parents who are authoritative anyway. For them, it's just another way to abuse power. In those cases, locking the young person out only worsens the problem.

Questions about the Family of an Addict

How can a wife be in submission to an addictive husband?

Submission to the *sins* of anyone in authority is not what's required in Scripture. To continue to tolerate his destructive behavior and be a nice person in the hope that he'll change is naive. What the wife is doing is making the way clear for him to continue to sin. The addictive mind reads that kind of submission as permission to continue the abuse.

What the Bible does ask the wife to do is respond to her husband's legitimate needs. That may mean confronting him with his sin so he can reconcile himself to God and finally to his family. She still honors the marriage vow and sees the goal of reconciliation as foremost.

Should I ever recommend that a spouse leave his or her addicted mate?

Leaving has the potential of becoming irreversible and should be recommended only if all else fails. First, advise the spouse to do things like confronting the situation, getting counseling himself or herself, and arranging an intervention. Leaving is necessary if it's obvious that grievous damage is being done—such as physical or sexual abuse and nothing else has worked. Leaving, however, doesn't mean filing for divorce. The whole family's well-being needs to be seriously considered—especially the children, who are subjected to life in such a painful environment.

If the husband or wife does leave, his or her stand should be, "If you're willing to confront your problems honestly and deal with them, I'm willing to come back and help, but only if you begin with actions and not just promises."

Matthew 18:15-17 doesn't teach reconciliation at any cost but after recognition of the harm done and a repentant response. This is one facet of real love in action.

Why can't the adult child of an alcoholic pray, read the Bible, confess his or her sin, and get over what happened?

The principles of the Word of God—confession, the relinquishment of control, a mind change that leads to changes in behavior such as self-acceptance—do lead to freedom.

But too often we treat spiritual disciplines as magic rituals: "Pray and read your Bibles enough, and that will fix whatever's wrong." Rather, it's how one applies what one receives that determines whether or not it's beneficial.

The steps followed by most support groups are based on biblical principles: making a deep examination of oneself, facing what's true and confessing it to others, exercising dependence on God. But the individual is doing it in community with others like himself or herself. By their very presence, others reinforce and augment the spiritual process.

How can the child of an addict stop hating a parent who abused him or her when drunk?

The first step is to face the situation and see it as it really was. The child of an abusive addict has to admit inside, "I really did experience this." The second step is to get in touch with the pain and grieve over the loss of a parent who wasn't what he or she should have been. Anger and hatred are often coverings for grief. Another key factor to keep in mind is that the child was helpless, but as an adult he or she can experience power and break the childhood bondage.

In some cases, the victim needs to get in touch with the abuser. It depends on the situation; contacting some parents could be destructive. An example is the father who is still a substance abuser and locked in the same self-serving mindset. Such a meeting could do more harm than good.

Whether or not a confrontation takes place, the victim can forgive and not carry around the effects. That doesn't mean the two will be reconciled. The victim can be open to it, but true reconciliation depends on whether the offender is living and what his or her attitude is now.

If a child in my church has an addicted parent at home but the nonaddicted parent won't confront the addict or get help, what can I do?

The best route is to visit in the home and assess the situation. Addicted families are usually protective about what goes on and remain isolated. To confront the abuser may mean that the child is withdrawn from church and you'll lose the contact you do have. Hopefully, through repeated contact, you can build a relationship with the parent.

However, if the child is being abused or neglected, you must report the situation to the authorities immediately. Doing so means you'll be instrumental in getting the child placed with another family and may help this family to face the problem.

Chapter One

1. Mark Miller, "Bennett's New Optimism," *Newsweek*, March 12, 1990, p. 32.

2. Most material taken from "A Glossary of Drug Related Terms," Horizon Recovery Center, Eugene, Oregon.

Chapter Four

1. Richard Mouw, "The Life of Bondage in the Light of Grace," *Christianity Today*, December 9, 1988, p. 41.

Chapter Five

1. *Al-Anon Family Groups*, (New York, NY: Al-Anon Family Group Headquarters, Inc., 1986), p. 112.

2. Janet Geringer Woititz, *Adult Children of Alcoholics* (Health Communications, Inc., 1983). This book provides more information on the subject.

3. "Liontamers," First Evangelical Free Church, 2801 North Brea Blvd., Fullerton, CA 92635-2799.

Appendix

The Twelve Steps

The Twelve Steps are reprinted with permission of Alcoholics Anonymous World Services, Inc. AA is for recovery from alcoholism only. There are other programs which address other problems and addictions.

Step One

"We admitted we were powerless over alcohol—that our lives had become unmanageable."

Step Two

"Came to believe that a Power greater than ourselves could restore us to sanity."

Step Three

"Made a decision to turn our will and our lives over to the care of God *as we understood Him*."

Step Four

"Made a searching and fearless moral inventory of ourselves."

Step Five

"Admitted to God, to ourselves, and to another human being the exact nature of our wrongs."

Step Six

"Were entirely ready to have God remove all these defects of character."

Step Seven
"Humbly asked Him to remove our shortcomings."

Step Eight
"Made a list of all persons we had harmed, and became willing to make amends to them all."

Step Nine
"Made direct amends to such people wherever possible, except when to do so would injure them or others."

Step Ten
"Continued to take personal inventory, and when we were wrong, promptly admitted it."

Step Eleven
"Sought through prayer and meditation to improve our conscious contact with God *as we understood Him*, praying only for knowledge of His will for us and the power to carry that out."

Step Twelve
"Having had a spiritual awakening as the result of these steps, we tried to carry this message to alcoholics, and to practice these principles in all our affairs."

BIBLIOGRAPHY

Books and other material listed may not be written from a Christian perspective. Read carefully and compare to your position as a Christian.

Books on Addiction

(Much of the material about alcoholism and its effects also applies to drug addiction.)

Alcoholics Anonymous, 1939. *Alcoholics Anonymous*. New York: Alcoholics Anonymous. Often called "The Big Book," it will inform you about the organization. Except for testimonies, it was written by Bill Wilson, cofounder of AA.

Alcoholics Anonymous, 1953. *Twelve Steps and Twelve Traditions*. New York: Alcoholics Anonymous. Discusses the principles on which AA is based. Also written by Bill Wilson.

Alcoholics Anonymous, 1975. *Living Sober*. New York: Alcoholics Anonymous. Describes techniques the organization's members have used to live without substance abuse.

Brecher, Edward M., and the editors of *Consumer Reports*, 1972. *Licit and Illicit Drugs*. Boston: Little Brown & Company. A comprehensive overview of drugs most often abused with a background of their introduction into society. Newer drugs not included, but still very helpful.

Brown, Stephanie, 1985. *Treating the Alcoholic: a Developmental Model of Recovery*. New York: John Wiley & Sons, Inc. Looks at addiction, particularly alcoholism as a developmental process with four phases: drinking, transition, early recovery, and ongoing recovery. Includes a clinical integration of Alcoholics Anonymous and psychotherapy. For the person who desires an in-depth clinical look at alcoholism.

Hart, Stan, 1988. *Rehab: a Comprehensive Guide to Recommended Drug-Alcohol Treatment Centers in the United States.* New York: Harper & Row, Publishers. An in-depth look at over a hundred treatment centers. While people you know may not go into one of these particular centers, the book provides valuable guidelines on questions to ask and what to look for in a good treatment center.

Rehrer, Ronald L., 1982. *Now What Do I Do?* St. Louis: Concordia. A guide on alcohol and drugs for a youth readership that is also helpful to parents and other adults.

Strack, Jay, 1985. *Drugs and Drinking.* Nashville: Thomas Nelson. Discusses symptoms, reasons for use by youth, gives an overview of drugs, and offers solutions to the problem of abuse.

Books about Families of Addicts

Al-Anon, 1973. *One Day at a Time in Al-Anon.* New York: Al-Anon Family Group Headquarters, Inc. Meditative thoughts and reminders for each day of the year designed to help the family member stay on track.

Black, Claudia, 1981. *It Will Never Happen to Me!* Denver: MAC Publishers. Explores the impact of alcoholism through personal stories and provides coping strategies.

Bradshaw, John, 1988. *The Family: a Revolutionary Way of Self-Discovery.* Pompano Beach, Florida: Health Communications. Vividly portrays how dysfunctional families create dysfunctional people. Good exploration of material but tends to get New Age oriented toward the end.

Wegsheider, Sharon, 1981. *Another Chance: Hope and Health for the Alcoholic Family.* Palo Alto, California: Science and Behavior Books. Clearly outlines the impact of alcoholism on each family member. Shows coping strategies and provides ideas for recovery.

Woititz, Janet Geringer, 1983. *Adult Children of Alcoholics*. Pompano Beach, Florida: Health Communications, Inc. Explains life as a child in a family controlled by addiction, the effects, results in the individual's life, and ways to break the cycle. Very popular.

Books for Children and Adolescents

Al-Anon, 1977. *What's "Drunk," Mama?* New York: Al-Anon Family Group Headquarters. Explores a young girl's feelings about her father's alcoholism. Told from a Twelve Step perspective.

Bissell, L., and Watherwax, R. 1982. *The Cat Who Drank Too Much*. Bantam, Connecticut: Bibulophile Press. Through the use of cats and their behavior, shows the problems and effects of alcoholism.

Black, Claudia, 1979. *My Dad Loves Me, My Dad Has a Disease: a Workbook for Children of Alcoholics*. Denver: MAC Publishers. Based on alcoholism as a disease. Very helpful in enabling children to learn about alcoholism as well as to express their feelings. Illustrated by children of alcoholics with blank pages for each child to draw his or her own pictures.

Hastings, Jill and Typpo, Marion, 1984. *An Elephant in the Living Room*. Minneapolis: CompCare Publishers. A workbook for children ages seven and up to help them learn about the disease of alcoholism as well as about self-esteem and decision-making. A good tool.

Jones, Penny, 1983. *The Brown Bottle*. Center City, Minnesota: Hazelden. A story about a caterpillar who becomes addicted to alcohol and doesn't recover.

Sanford, Doris and Evans, Graci, 1987. *I Know the World's Worst Secret: a Child's Book about Living with an Alcoholic Parent*. Portland, Oregon: Multnomah Press. A beautifully illustrated story of a young girl who tries to care for an alcoholic mother. Includes suggestions for adults on how to help.

Films and Videos

Another Chance. Health Communications, 3201 S.W. 15th St., Deerfield Beach, FL 33442. Featuring Sharon Wegscheider-Cruse. Focuses on issues affecting adult children of alcoholics.

The Cat Who Drank Too Much. FMS Productions, P.O. Box 4428, 520 East Montecito St., Suite F, Santa Barbara, CA 93140. Adaptation of the book by the same name. See description under books.

A Story about Feelings. The Johnson Institute, 7151 Metro Blvd., Minneapolis, MN 55435. Animated children's video showing how addiction affects feelings and how to feel good without drugs. Excellent for younger children.

Lots of Kids Like Us. Gerald T. Rogers Productions, Inc., 5225 Old Orchard Rd., Suite 6, Skokie, IL 60077. A wonderful film focusing on children of alcoholics and how they cannot cause, control, or cure the disease in their parents.

My Father's Son. Gerald T. Rogers Productions, Inc., 5225 Old Orchard Rd., Suite 6, Skokie, IL 60077. Looks at life from the point of view of a teenager from an addicted home. Explores the intergenerational impact of alcoholism.

Soft Is the Heart of a Child. Operation Cork/PGP, 138 B Ave., Coronado, CA 92118. Vividly portrays the different roles children adopt to survive in an alcoholic home.

Adult Children of Alcoholics: the Masks of Denial. Barr Films, 12801 Schabarum Ave., P.O. Box 7878, Irwindale, CA 91706-7878. A dramatization of the emotional and psychological problems faced by adult children of alcoholics. Portrays the four coping roles.

Organizations about Addiction

Write these groups for listings of material available:

Alcoholics Anonymous, P.O. Box 459, Grand Central Station, New York, NY 10163.

Alcoholics Victorious, P.O. Box 10364, Portland, OR 97210.

American Council on Alcoholism, White Marsh Business Center, 5024 Campbell Blvd., Suite H, Baltimore, MD 21236.

Cocaine Anonymous World Central Office, 6125 Washington Blvd., Suite 202, Culver City, CA 92030.

Just Say No Foundation, 1777 North California Blvd., Suite 210, Walnut Creek, CA 94596.

Life Skills Ed, 280 Broad St., Weymouth, Mass 02188.

National Association on Drug Abuse Problems, 355 Lexington Ave., New York, NY 10017.

Narcotics Anonymous, P.O. Box 9999, Van Nuys, CA 91409.

National Clearinghouse for Alcohol and Drug Information, P.O. Box 2345, Rockville, MD 20852.

National Council on Alcoholism, Inc., 12 W. 21st St., New York, NY 10010.

National Federation of Parents for Drug-Free Youth, 8730 Georgia Ave., Suite 200, Silver Springs, MD 20910.

National Institute on Alcohol Abuse and Alcoholism, 5600 Fishers Lane, Rockville, MD 20852.

NFP (National Federation of Parents for Drug-Free Youth), 1820 Franwell Ave., Suite 16, Silver Springs, MD 20902. Provides information on forming parent groups to combat problems of drugs in neighborhoods, schools, or communities. Could also be adapted by churches.

PRIDE (National Parents' Resource Institute for Drug Education), 100 Edgewood Ave., Suite 1216, Atlanta, GA 30303.

Public Affairs Committee, 381 Park Ave. S., New York, NY 10016.

Teen Challenge, Inc., 444 Clinton Ave., Brooklyn, NY 11238.

Women for Sobriety, P.O. Box 618, Quakertown, PA 18951.

(Also contact your local drug and alcohol abuse prevention agency.)

Organizations for Families of Addicts

Al-Anon/Alateen Family Group Headquarters, Inc., P.O. Box 182, Madison Square Station, New York, NY 10159-0182.

Children of Alcoholics Foundation, Inc., 31st floor, 200 Park Ave., New York, NY 10166.

Codependents Anonymous, National Service Office, P.O. Box 5508, Glendale, AZ 85313-5508.

Families Anonymous, P.O. Box 528, Van Nuys, CA 91408.

National Association for Children of Alcoholics, 31582 Coast Hwy., Suite B, South Laguna, CA 92677.

(See *The Encyclopedia of Associations* in the reference section of your library for organizations that specialize in particular subgroups, such as addicted physicians or attorneys.)

Newsletters

Alateen Talk, P.O. Box 182, Madison Square Station, New York, NY 10159-0182. Bimonthly newsletter detailing events, conferences, and sponsors.

Grapevine, P.O. Box 459, Grand Central Station, New York, NY 10163. Monthly Alcoholics Anonymous journal.

NACA Network, 31582 Coast Highway, Suite B, South Laguna, CA 92677. Quarterly newsletter for the National Association for Children of Alcoholics, detailing research and conferences.

Prevention Parentline, The Editor, NFP, 8730 Georgia Ave., Suite 200, Silver Springs, MD 20910. Quarterly newsletter of the National Federation of Parents for Drug Free Youth.

(Other organizations also publish newsletters. Ask for information when you write.)

For Help in Starting a Support Group

Write for information available and cost.

Bob Bartosch, Overcomers Outreach, Inc., 2290 West Whittier Blvd., Suite D, La Habra, CA 90631.

New Hope Community Church, 11731 S.E. Stevens Rd., Portland, OR 97266.

First Evangelical Free Church, 2801 North Brea Blvd., Fullerton, CA 92635-2799.

Periodicals

"Alcohol and the Family," *Newsweek* (January 18, 1988), pp. 62-68. Overview of problems of children of alcoholics and their recovery.

Alsdurf, Phyllis; Alsdurf, Jim; Bird, Brian; Hart, Archibald, "Getting Free," *Christianity Today* (December 9, 1988). Addiction and codependency in Christian perspective.

"Hour by Hour: Crack," *Newsweek* (November 28, 1988), pp. 64-75. Describes crack use and the law in major U.S. cities.

"How to Beat Drugs." *U.S. News and World Report* (September 11, 1989): 69-86. A family guide to prevention, treatment, and community action.

"Unite and Conquer," *Newsweek* (February 5, 1990), pp. 50-55. A review of the support groups—many based on the Twelve Steps—that are used by 15 million Americans.